SECOND EDITION

Constructing Achievement Tests

Norman E. Gronlund

PROFESSOR OF EDUCATIONAL PSYCHOLOGY
UNIVERSITY OF ILLINOIS

PRENTICE-HALL, INC., Englewood Cliffs, N.J. 07632

Library of Congress Cataloging in Publication Data

GRONLUND, NORMAN EDWARD (date)
Constructing achievement tests.

Includes bibliographies and index.
1. Educational tests and measurements. I. Title.
LB3051.G73 1977 371.26'42 76-56199
ISBN 0-13-169235-6

Printed in the United States of America

10 9 8 7 6 5 4 3 2

PRENTICE-HALL INTERNATIONAL, INC., *London*
PRENTICE-HALL OF AUSTRALIA PTY. LIMITED, *Sydney*
PRENTICE-HALL OF CANADA, LTD., *Toronto*
PRENTICE-HALL OF INDIA PRIVATE LIMITED, *New Delhi*
PRENTICE-HALL OF JAPAN, INC., *Tokyo*
PRENTICE-HALL OF SOUTHEAST ASIA PTE. LTD., *Singapore*
WHITEHALL BOOKS LIMITED, *Wellington, New Zealand*

To Ida, Leda, Marie, and Erik

Contents

Preface

This second edition of *Constructing Achievement Tests* incorporates several important changes. First, new material on the preparation and use of *criterion-referenced tests* (that is, tests designed to describe the learning tasks students can perform) has been added to various chapters. Second, a completely new chapter on performance testing (Chapter 6) has been added. Third, greater emphasis has been given to the use of achievement tests in the instructional process. Fourth, the chapter on test interpretation (Chapter 8) and the chapter on validity and reliability (Chapter 9) have been revised to incorporate new material on criterion-referenced testing. With these changes, the book now provides a fairly well-balanced treatment of the preparation, use, and evaluation of criterion-referenced and norm-referenced achievement tests.

Like the first edition, this edition is intended for teachers and prospective teachers at all levels of education, and for others who are responsible for constructing achievement tests. A basic theme of the book is that achievement tests should be designed to measure clearly defined learning outcomes (that is, instructional objectives) and the results should be used to guide and improve student learning.

The chapters on test planning and test construction use Benjamin S. Bloom's *Taxonomy of Educational Objectives: Cognitive Domain* as a basic frame of reference, and the illustrative test items are keyed to the Taxonomy categories. This source and its companion volumes on the affective and psychomotor domains are listed at the end of Chapter 2.

In an attempt to make the sample test items more meaningful to teachers in various instructional areas, I have based them on the material in this book. When a sample item is introduced, only the content that has already been discussed is included in the item. This clarifies the relation between subject matter and test content in a way that would not otherwise be possible. Although the sample test items may also provide some review of the material presented earlier, I made no attempt to use these items to provide a systematic review of all previous material.

Since I wrote this book as a practical guide for the test maker, I made special efforts to keep the writing direct and understandable. No previous training in either measurement or statistics is needed to comprehend the material. The methods of interpreting test scores and the material on validity and reliability can be understood by anyone with a knowledge of arithmetic. For those who wish more information on a particular topic, lists of selected references are appended to each chapter.

I wish to express special thanks to the authors and publishers referred to in the text, for their contributions. The efficient typing services of Marian Brinkerhoff are also gratefully acknowledged.

Norman E. Gronlund

1

Achievement Testing as an Aid to Learning

Achievement tests should support and reinforce other aspects of the instructional process. They can aid both the teacher and the student in assessing learning readiness . . . monitoring learning progress . . . diagnosing learning difficulties . . . and evaluating learning outcomes. . . . The effectiveness of testing is enhanced by observing a set of basic principles. . . . and by noting the differences between norm-referenced and criterion-referenced tests.

Achievement testing plays a prominent role in all types of instructional programs. It is the most widely used method of assessing pupil achievement in classroom instruction, and it is an indispensable procedure in individualized and programmed instruction. Despite the widespread use of achievement testing and its importance in evaluating and guiding student learning, many teachers receive little or no training in how to construct good achievement tests. This book is an attempt to remedy that deficiency. It places major emphasis on the principles and procedures of test construction that are useful to classroom teachers.

An achievement test is a systematic procedure for determining the amount a student has learned. Although the emphasis is on measuring learning outcomes, it should not be implied that testing is to be done only at the end of instruction. All too frequently, achievement testing is viewed as an end-of-unit or end-of-course activity that is used primarily for assigning course grades. Although this is a necessary and useful function of testing, it is just one of many. As with teaching, the main purpose of testing is to improve learning, and within this larger context there are a number of specific contributions it can make.

Testing in the Instructional Process

In order to realize the full potential of achievement tests as learning aids, it is necessary to make testing an integral part of the instructional process. Testing should be considered during the planning for instruction, and it should play a significant role in the various stages of instruction. From the beginning of instruction to the end, there are numerous decisions that teachers must make. Testing can improve the effectiveness of many of these decisions by providing more objective information on which to base the judgments.

Let us consider three types of decisions teachers need to make that can be aided by testing: (1) decisions at the beginning of instruction, (2) decisions during instruction, and (3) decisions at the end of instruction. Doing so will also help acquaint us with the names of the test types that are typically associated with each stage of instruction.

BEGINNING OF INSTRUCTION (PLACEMENT TESTING)

There are two major questions that teachers need to answer before proceeding with the instruction:

1. To what extent do the students possess the skills and abilities that are needed to begin instruction?
2. To what extent have the students already achieved the intended learning outcomes of the planned instruction?

Information concerning the first question can be obtained from *readiness* pretests. These are tests given at the beginning of a course, or unit of instruction, that cover those prerequisite skills considered necessary for success in the planned instruction. For example, a test of computational skill might be given at the beginning of an algebra course, or a test of English grammar might be given at the beginning of a German course. Students lacking in prerequisite skills could be given remedial work, or they could be placed in a special section that had lower prerequisites.

The second question can be answered by a *placement* pretest covering the intended learning outcomes of the planned instruction. This might very well be the same test that is given at the end of the instruction; preferably, it should be another form of it. Here we are interested in determining whether students have already mastered some of the material we plan to include in our instruction. If they have, we might need to modify our teaching plans, encourage some students to skip particular units, and place other students at a more advanced level of instruction.

Placement testing is, of course, not always necessary. Teachers who have worked with students for some time may know their past achievements well enough that a pretest at the beginning of an instructional unit is not needed. In other cases, a course or unit of instruction may not have a clearly defined set of prerequisite skills. Similarly, some areas of instruction may be so new to the students that it can be assumed that none of the students have achieved the intended outcomes of the planned instruction. Placement testing is probably most useful when the teacher is unfamiliar with the students' skills and abilities, and when the intended outcomes of instruction can be clearly specified and organized in meaningful sequences. Under these conditions, the placement test provides an invaluable aid for placing each student at the most beneficial position in the instructional sequence.

DURING INSTRUCTION (FORMATIVE AND DIAGNOSTIC TESTING)

During the instructional program our main concern is with the learning progress being made by students. Questions such as the following must be answered:

1. On which learning tasks are the students progressing satisfactorily? On which ones do they need help?
2. Which students are having such severe learning problems that they need remedial work?

Tests used to monitor student progress during instruction are called *formative* tests (see Bloom, Hastings, and Madaus, 1971; Gronlund, 1976).* Formative tests are typically designed to measure the extent to which students have mastered the learning outcomes of a rather limited segment of instruction, such as a unit or a textbook chapter. These tests are similar to the quizzes and unit tests that teachers have traditionally

*Text references are cited fully at the end of each chapter.

used, but they place greater emphasis on (1) measuring all of the intended outcomes of the unit of instruction, and (2) using the results to improve learning (rather than to assign grades). The purpose is to identify the students' learning successes and failures so that adjustments in instruction and learning can be made. When the majority of students fail a test item, or set of items, the material is typically retaught in a group setting. When a minority of students experience learning failures, alternate methods of study are usually prescribed for each student (for example, reading assignments in a second book, programmed instruction, and visual aids). These corrective prescriptions are frequently keyed to each item, or to each set of items designed to measure a separate learning task, so that students can begin immediately after testing to correct their individual learning errors.

When a student's learning problems are so persistent that they cannot be resolved by the corrective prescriptions of formative testing, a more intensive study of the student's learning difficulties is called for. It is here that the *diagnostic* test is useful. This type of test typically includes a relatively large number of test items in each specific area, with slight variations from one item to the next so that the cause of specific learning errors can be identified. The diagnostic test attempts to answer such questions as the following: Is the student having difficulty in addition because he doesn't know certain number combinations or because he doesn't know how to carry? Is the student's difficulty in reading German due to his inadequate knowledge of vocabulary or to his poor grasp of certain elements of grammar? Is the student unable to apply scientific principles to new situations because he doesn't understand the principles, because his knowledge of particular concepts is weak, or because the new situations are too unfamiliar to him? Thus, the diagnostic test focuses on the common sources of error encountered by students, so that the learning difficulties can be pinpointed and remedied.

Diagnosing learning problems is a matter of degree. The formative test determines whether a student has mastered the learning tasks being taught, and, if not, prescribes how to remedy the learning failures. The diagnostic test is designed to probe deeper into the causes of learning deficiencies that are left unresolved by formative testing. Of course, this is not to imply that all learning problems can be overcome by formative and diagnostic testing. These are simply tools to aid in the identification and diagnosis of specific learning difficulties so that appropriate remedial steps can be taken. Diagnosing and remedying severe learning problems frequently requires a wide array of evaluative tools and the services of specially trained personnel. All we are attempting to do here is to show how formative and diagnostic tests can contribute to improved student learning during instruction.

END OF INSTRUCTION (SUMMATIVE TESTING)

At the end of a course or unit of instruction we are concerned primarily with the extent to which the students have achieved the intended outcomes of the instruction. Questions such as the following must be answered:

1. Which students have mastered the learning tasks to such a degree that they should proceed to the next course or unit of instruction?
2. What grade should be assigned to each student?

The achievement test given at the end of a period of instruction for the purpose of certifying mastery or assigning grades is called a *summative* test (see Bloom, Hastings, and Madaus, 1971; Gronlund, 1976). These tests are typically broad in coverage and attempt to measure a representative sample of all of the learning tasks included in the instruction. Although the results are used primarily for grading, they can contribute to greater future learning by providing information for evaluating the effectiveness of the instruction.

Other Ways Tests Influence Learning

In addition to improving instructional decisions, the use of tests can aid learning by (1) improving student motivation, (2) increasing retention and transfer of learning, (3) increasing student self-understanding, and (4) providing feedback concerning instructional effectiveness. Each of these will be discussed in turn.

TESTS AID STUDENT MOTIVATION

Periodic testing motivates students by providing them with short-term goals toward which to work, by clarifying for them what learning outcomes are expected, and by providing them with feedback concerning their learning progress. The anticipation of a test arouses greater learning activity, and the nature of the expected test channels and directs the type of learning that takes place. Although this influence of testing is sometimes considered undesirable, as when the test measures only the recall of facts, it need not be a negative influence. Its contribution to, or detraction from, improved learning depends largely on how faithfully our tests reflect the learning outcomes we want our students to achieve and how we use the results. If the "application of principles" is stressed in our testing, as well as in our teaching, we can expect students to direct greater efforts toward learning how to apply principles. Also, if the test results are reported to students as soon as possible, this feedback concerning their strengths and weaknesses in the "application of principles" will further clarify the nature of the task and indicate what changes are needed for effective performance. Thus, properly constructed tests can motivate students to work toward the instructional objectives of a course by arousing greater learning activity, by directing it toward the desired learning outcomes, and by providing prompt knowledge of results.

TESTS AID RETENTION AND TRANSFER OF LEARNING

Since tests tend to direct students' learning efforts toward the objectives being measured, they can be used as tools for increasing the retention and transfer of classroom learning. In general, learning outcomes at the understanding, application, and interpretation levels are likely to be retained longer and to have greater transfer value than outcomes at the knowledge level. By including measures of these more complex learning outcomes in our tests, we can direct attention to their importance and provide reinforcing practice in the comprehension skills, applications, and interpretations we are attempting to develop. Thus, tests can be used to supplement and complement our teaching efforts in these areas and thereby increase the likelihood that the learning will be of greater permanent value to the students.

TESTS AID STUDENT SELF-UNDERSTANDING

A major aim of all instruction is to help individuals understand themselves better so that they can make more intelligent decisions and evaluate their performance more effectively. Periodic testing and feedback of the results can help students gain insight into the things they can do well, the misconceptions that need correction, the degree of skill they have in various areas, and the like. Such information provides the student with a more objective basis for planning a study program, for selecting future educational experiences, and for developing self-evaluation skills. Properly constructed tests tend to provide evidence of learning progress in such an objective and impartial way that the results can be accepted with little resistance or distortion. This assumes, of course, that the tests are being used to improve learning and not to threaten or label students. In the latter instance, self-understanding is apt to be distorted by the defense mechanisms an individual uses to maintain a positive self-image.

TESTS PROVIDE FEEDBACK CONCERNING INSTRUCTIONAL EFFECTIVENESS

Information provided by test results can be used to evaluate various aspects of the instructional process. It can help determine the extent to which the instructional objectives were realistic, whether the methods and materials of instruction were appropriate, and how well the learning experiences were organized. Test results not only reveal the learning weaknesses of individual students; they can also reveal weaknesses in instruction when the results of the group are considered as a whole. When the majority of the students do poorly on the same test items, it may be the fault of the students, but the difficulty is more apt to be found in the instruction. The teacher may be striving for learning outcomes that are unattainable by the students, or he may be using ineffective methods for bringing about the desired changes (assuming the test is suitable, of course). The students' responses to the test and the post-test discussion of the results should provide clues to the source of the instructional difficulty, and corrective steps can thereby be taken.

Basic Principles of Achievement Testing

The extent to which achievement tests contribute to improved learning and instruction is determined largely by the principles underlying their development and use. Tests can direct students' attention toward the objectives of instruction or away from time. They can encourage students to focus on a limited aspect of the course content or direct their attention to all of the important areas. They can reward superficial learning or require deep understanding. They can provide dependable information for instructional decisions, or they can provide biased and distorted information. The following principles of achievement testing provide a firm base for constructing and using classroom tests as a positive force in the teaching-learning process.

1. Achievement tests should measure clearly defined learning outcomes that are in harmony with the instructional objectives. Achievement tests can be designed to measure a variety of learning outcomes, such as the knowledge of specific facts, the knowledge of terms, an understanding of concepts and principles, the ability to apply facts and principles, and various thinking skills. The first order of business in constructing an achievement test, then, is not the construction of test items, but rather the identification and definition of the learning outcomes to be measured. These should logically grow out of the instructional objectives of the course in which the test is to be used. The sequence of steps for determining the learning outcomes is as follows:

1. Identify the instructional objectives of the course.
2. State the objectives in terms of general learning outcomes (for instance, "Student understands the meaning of common terms").
3. Under each objective, list the *specific* learning outcomes you are willing to accept as evidence of the attainment of that objective. These should also be stated in terms of observable behavior (for example, "Student can (a) define terms in his own words, (b) distinguish between terms on the basis of meaning, and (c) use the terms effectively in original sentences").

If this sequence of steps is carried out properly, the specific learning outcomes will indicate clearly what behavior should be measured by the test in order to reflect the objectives of the instruction adequately. When stated clearly in behavioral terms, these steps also suggest the type of test items to use. If you expect students to be able to "define terms in their own words," for example, simply give them the terms and direct them to write definitions. A true-false or multiple-choice item would obviously not call forth the specific behavior described in this learning outcome.

In summary, achievement tests measure the specific behaviors students are expected to demonstrate at the end of a learning experience. In order for the tests to be most useful these learning outcomes should be clearly defined and should faithfully reflect the instructional objectives of the course. This procedure is such an important phase of achievement testing that a portion of the next chapter will be devoted to a detailed description of it.

2. Achievement tests should measure a representative sample of the learning outcomes and subject matter included in the instruction. Testing is always a matter of sampling. We can never ask all of the questions we would like to ask in a test. At the end of a learning experience there may be hundreds of facts and terms we expect students to know, but because of the time available for testing, and other considerations, we can include only enough items to measure a fraction of these facts. Or, we might complete a unit of instruction containing principles that have innumerable applications to specific situations, but we can measure only a given number of these applications. Thus, tests always provide a somewhat limited sample of the behavior we are interested in measuring. It is the responsibility of the test user to determine how adequately the sample in the test reflects the universe of situations it is supposed to represent.

One way to be more sure that an achievement test provides a representative sample of the desired behavior is to use a table of specifications. This is a twofold table in which the learning outcomes are listed on one side and the subject-matter topics on the other. The intersecting cells in the table make it possible to indicate the proportion of the test to be devoted to each learning outcome and each subject-matter topic. A simplified version of this instrument is presented in Table 1.1. More detailed descriptions of the development and use of a table of specifications will appear in the next chapter.

Although the table of specifications is a useful device, its effectiveness depends largely on how adequately the learning outcomes and sub-

Table 1.1. *Table of Specifications for a Unit in Test Construction*

LEARNING OUTCOMES / SUBJECT-MATTER TOPICS	KNOWLEDGE OF FACTS AND PRINCIPLES	UNDERSTANDING OF FACTS AND PRINCIPLES	APPLICATION OF FACTS AND PRINCIPLES	TOTAL NUMBER OF ITEMS
1. Planning the test	5*	5		10
2. Constructing objective test items	5	10	10	25
3. Constructing essay questions	5	5	5	15
4. Assembling the test	10	5	15	30
5. Using and appraising the test	5	5	10	20
Total number of items	30	30	40	100

* Either the number of items or the percentage of items may be recorded in each cell.

ject-matter topics have been described. If an achievement test is to serve as a comprehensive summative measure of achievement in a course, the learning outcomes should cover all instructional objectives that can be tested, and the subject-matter topics should include all of the major content areas that were considered during the course. These can then be weighted in importance, and a corresponding number of items can be allotted to each cell. Thus, to adequately sample the achievement in a course, the test should reflect the emphasis in the table of specifications, which in turn should reflect the emphasis during instruction.

3. ***Achievement tests should include the types of test items that are most appropriate for measuring the desired learning outcomes.*** The learning outcomes for a course specify the types of behavior we are willing to accept as evidence of the achievement of the instructional objectives. The achievement test is simply a device for calling forth the specified behavior so that judgments can be made concerning the extent to which learning has taken place. The key to effective achievement testing, then, is to select the most appropriate item-type and to construct it so carefully that it elicits the desired response and precludes other irrelevant responses. This is the ideal situation, of course, and we can only approximate it in classroom testing.

The extent to which students' responses to test items can be controlled varies with the type of item used. The major classifications of achievement-test items are as follows:

A. Supply-type (student supplies answer)
  (1) Essay—extended response
  (2) Essay—restricted response
  (3) Short answer (word or phrase)
  (4) Completion (fill in blanks)
B. Selection-type (student selects answer)
  (1) True-false (or alternate response)
  (2) Matching
  (3) Multiple-choice

Supply-type items present a less structured task than selection-type items; consequently, it is more difficult to control the nature of the student's response. The greatest difficulty is encountered with the extended-response essay question. This type of question is general in nature (for example, "Describe the role of measurement and evaluation in teaching"), and permits the student almost unlimited freedom in selecting the factual information to include, in organizing his answer, and in relating and evaluating the ideas included. Thus, the extended-response essay may be useful for measuring such general learning outcomes as "the ability to select relevant material," "the ability to organize ideas," and "the ability to evaluate ideas," but it is of little value for measuring specific responses. It is inappropriate for measuring knowledge of certain facts or particular types of understanding, for example, as these may or may not appear in the answer—because of the amount of freedom given the writer. Although a certain amount of control over the student's response can be obtained through the directions (in regard to length of answer, time limit, and so forth), for the measurement of more specific learning outcomes it is usually necessary to use a more structured item type.

The restricted-response essay (for example, "Describe two advantages and two limitations of the extended-response essay question") limits the generality, length, and organization of the student's answer. Note that this control over the student's response makes the item more useful as a measure of the understanding of specific facts, but inappropriate as a measure of "the ability to organize ideas." This illustrates the importance of selecting the item type that is most appropriate for measuring the desired learning outcomes.

The remaining supply-type items provide even greater structuring of the student's response. Since short-answer and completion items require the student to supply only a word or a phrase, they are limited almost entirely to the measurement of knowledge outcomes, such as the recall of specific facts.

Selection-type items provide the greatest structure, and they can be used to measure a variety of learning outcomes, from simple to complex. True-false items consist of propositions concerning such things as facts, principles, laws, applications, and interpretations; the student is requested to indicate whether the propositions are true or false. Matching exercises present a set of premises and responses to be matched. These may be terms and definitions, rules and examples, principles and illustrations of the principles, and the like. Multiple-choice items present a problem, or question, and several alternative solutions from which the student must select the correct response. These alternatives may be factual statements, illustrations of a procedure, examples of a principle, or any other type of response. Note that despite the specific nature of each selection-type exercise, the type of response the student can make to any of them is limited. He must correctly identify a proposition as true or false, match a premise with the correct response, or select the correct answer from a set of plausible solutions to a problem. He is not free to redefine the problem, provide partially correct answers, or demonstrate learnings irrelevant to those demanded by the test items. Thus, the greater control afforded by selection-type exercises increases the likelihood that the responses called forth by the test items will match those reflected in the learning outcomes to be measured.

4. Achievement tests should be designed to fit the particular uses to be made of the results. As we noted earlier, achievement tests may be used for a variety of purposes. They may be used to measure students' (1) entry behavior at the beginning of instruction (placement test), (2) learning progress during instruction (formative test), (3) causes of learning difficulties during instruction (diagnostic test), and (4) general achievement at the end of instruction (summative test).

The placement pretest designed to measure prerequisite skills typically has a low level of difficulty and is rather narrow in scope. It may cover the minimum essentials of a prerequisite unit of instruction, or some other limited set of required skills. For example, a test of addition might be given at the beginning of a unit on multiplication, or a test of basic statistical procedures might be given at the beginning of a course in research methods. In contrast with this limited measure of prerequisite skills, the placement pretest designed to measure which intended outcomes of the planned instruction the students have already achieved is broad in scope. It is, in fact, no different from the summative test given at the end of instruction.

The formative test, used to monitor learning progress, is designed to cover a limited segment of instruction—say, a unit or chapter—and attempts to measure all important outcomes of that segment. The emphasis is on measuring mastery of the learning tasks and providing feedback to students concerning specific learning errors in areas where mastery has not been achieved. Thus, the formative test consists of a comprehensive set of specific test items concerning a limited area of instruction. It is constructed in such a way that students can be given specific prescriptions for correcting the errors revealed by missed items. Since these are learning tests, they typically have a lower level of difficulty than the summative tests given at the end of instruction.

The diagnostic test contains a relatively large number of items for each specific area being tested. Since the purpose of the test is to pinpoint learning difficulties, attention is focused on the students' responses to specific items, or groups of items, and the total score is of only minor importance. The test usually focuses on the common errors students make, rather than attempting to sample broadly the intended learning outcomes of the instruction. In a test of grammatical usage, for example, a series of sentences using "lay" or "lie" might be used to determine the specific situations that are causing each student difficulty. Since these tests are designed for those with learning problems, they tend to have a low level of difficulty.

The summative test (or general survey test) is designed to measure the broad range of learning outcomes expected at the end of instruction. Comprehensiveness and representativeness of sampling are important features of this test, since the results are to be used for assigning grades or for certifying mastery of the instructional objectives. In order to adequately sample all of the intended outcomes of instruction, the summative test typically contains items that exhibit a wider range of difficulty than the other test types.

The principles and procedures of test construction are similar for these various types of tests, but the sample of material included in the test and the difficulty of the test items must be modified to fit the particular uses to be made of the results.

5. Achievement tests should be made as reliable as possible and should then be interpreted with caution. If the scores students receive on an achievement test agree closely with those they would receive on a second administration of the same test, or an equivalent form of the test, the scores would be considered highly reliable. All test scores contain some error (due to variations in the testing conditions, in the students' responses, and so forth), but the proportionate amount of error can be reduced considerably by proper test construction. In general, the reliability of a test can be increased by lengthening the test and by improving the quality of each test item. Longer tests provide a more adequate sample of the behavior being measured, and properly constructed test items provide a more dependable description of each individual's test performance.

When the purpose of achievement testing is to obtain a relative ranking of students (for instance, for relative grading), greater reliability can be obtained by constructing a test that provides a wide range of test scores. This is typically accomplished by writing items at the 50-percent level of difficulty (50 percent of the students obtain correct answers) and by paying close attention to how well each item discriminates between high and low achievers. Procedures for determining item difficulty and item discriminating power will be discussed in Chapter 7. Here it is sufficient to point out that for a reliable ranking of students, a relatively large spread of test scores is needed.

When the purpose of testing is to describe which learning tasks each student can and cannot perform, rather than to rank students in order of achievement, the range of test scores is irrelevant. In this situation, item difficulty is determined by the difficulty of the learning task to be measured, and no attempt is made to manipulate item difficulty to obtain a spread of scores. Since the traditional estimates of test reliability are based on score variability, special problems are encountered when constructing reliable tests that do not require score variability. Here we must depend more heavily on matching the test items as closely as possible to the specific learning tasks, using a sufficient number of items for each learning task, and writing items that clearly call forth the desired behavior.

Despite the care taken during test construction, the test results will contain a certain amount of measurement error. The instructor must take this error into account during test interpretation. Procedures for doing so will be considered in Chapter 9.

6. Achievement tests should be used to improve student learning. This, of course, has been the theme of this entire chapter. Earlier, we pointed out that achievement tests can aid in instructional decisions, can directly influence the student's learning, and can provide information concerning teaching effectiveness. In this section, we have emphasized those principles of achievement testing that should enhance its value as a learning device. In summary, achievement tests will have the greatest positive influence on learning when they faithfully reflect the instructional objectives, when they measure an adequate sample of the intended learning outcomes, when they include item types most appropriate for the learning outcomes, when they are adapted to the particular uses to be made of the results, and when they are designed to yield reliable results.

In addition to the above factors, it is important to communicate to the students, by both word and deed, that the main purpose of testing is to improve their learning. Pointing out the relationship between the instructional objectives and the types of tests used, clarifying the nature and scope of all tests before they are given, providing feedback on the students' test performance as soon as possible following testing, and making specific suggestions concerning needed improvement—all of these are positive steps that can be taken. These and similar procedures should cause students to view tests as helpful tools and should increase the extent to which testing reinforces other experiences in the teaching-learning process.

Norm-Referenced Versus Criterion-Referenced Testing

As we noted earlier, an achievement test can be used to provide (1) a relative ranking of students, or (2) a description of the learning tasks a student can and cannot perform. Test results of the first type are interpreted in terms of each student's relative standing among other students (for example, "He is third highest in a class of thirty-five students"). This method of interpreting test performance is called *norm-referenced* interpretation. Test results of the second type are expressed in terms of the specific knowledges and skills each student can demonstrate (for instance, "He can identify all parts of the microscope and demonstrate its proper use"). This method of interpreting test results is called *criterion-referenced* interpretation. Both methods of describing test results are useful. The first tells how an individual's test performance compares with that of others. The second tells, in specific performance terms, what an individual can do, without reference to the performance of others.

Strictly speaking, the terms *norm reference* and *criterion reference* refer only to the method of interpreting test results. Thus, both types of interpretation could be applied to the same test. For example, we might say, "Joan surpassed 90 percent of the students (norm-referenced interpretation) by correctly completing twenty of the twenty-five chemical equations" (criterion-referenced interpretation). The two types of test interpretation are likely to be most meaningful, however, when the test is designed specifically for the type of interpretation to be made. In general, norm-referenced interpretation is facilitated by tests that provide a wide spread of scores so that reliable discriminations can be made among students at various levels of achievement. This is typically done by eliminating easy test items and favoring items of average difficulty. On the other hand, criterion-referenced interpretation is facilitated by including test items that are directly relevant to the learning outcomes, whether or not they are easy for students. Eliminating the easy items would provide incomplete descriptions of student performance because such descriptions would not include those learning tasks that were mastered by *all* students. Since each type of interpretation is favored by a different approach to test construction, the terms *norm-referenced test* and *criterion-referenced test* have come into widespread use.

CONSTRUCTING NORM-REFERENCED AND CRITERION-REFERENCED TESTS

There are more similarities than differences in the preparation of norm-referenced tests (NRTs) and criterion-referenced tests (CRTs), and the differences are largely a matter of emphasis. The following summary highlights the major similarities and differences in constructing NRTs and CRTs for measuring achievement.

1. Both typically require the specification of objectives (intended learning outcomes) as a basis for test construction.
   NRT: the objectives may be stated in general or specific terms.
   CRT: the objectives tend to be highly specific and detailed.
2. Both are typically designed to measure a representative sample of the

specified learning outcomes (for instance, by means of a table of specifications).

NRT: usually, a broad range of outcomes is covered, with few items per outcome.

CRT: usually, a limited domain of outcomes is covered, with numerous items per outcome.

3. Both use a variety of types of test items.

NRT: selection-type items are highly favored.

CRT: there is less dependence on selection-type items.

4. Both require the application of a common set of rules for effective item writing.

NRT: the ability of items to *discriminate* among students is emphasized.

CRT: the ability of items to *describe* student performance on specific learning tasks is emphasized.

5. Both require attention to the reliability of the results.

NRT: the traditional statistical procedures for estimating reliability are appropriate (because of high score variability).

CRT: the traditional statistical procedures for estimating reliability are inappropriate (due to possible lack of score variability—see Chapter 9).

6. Both are constructed to fit a particular use.

NRT: used primarily in advanced placement and summative testing.

CRT: used primarily in readiness, formative, and diagnostic testing.

Most of the discussions of test construction in the following chapters will apply to both test types. Where there are significant differences in the procedures of test development, these will be pointed out.

Additional Reading

Bloom, B. S., J. T. Hastings, and G. F. Madaus, *Handbook on Formative and Summative Evaluation of Student Learning*, Chaps. 4–6. New York: McGraw-Hill Book Company, 1971. Comprehensive treatment of summative, placement, diagnostic, and formative evaluation.

Glaser, R., and A. J. Nitko, "Measurement in Learning and Instruction," in *Educational Measurement* (2nd ed.), ed. R. L. Thorndike, Chap. 17. Washington, D.C.: American Council on Education, 1971. Comprehensive and systematic treatment of the topic.

Gronlund, N. E., *Measurement and Evaluation in Teaching* (3rd ed.), Chap. 1. New York: Macmillan Publishing Co., Inc., 1976. An overview of the principles and procedures of educational testing and evaluation.

———, *Preparing Criterion-Referenced Tests for Classroom Instruction.* New York: Macmillan Publishing Co., Inc., 1973. A brief book (55 pages) describing the nature and construction of criterion-referenced tests.

PAYNE, D. A., *The Assessment of Learning,* Chap. 13. Lexington, Mass.: D. C. Heath and Co., 1974. Describes and illustrates criterion-referenced tests.

POPHAM, W. J., *Educational Evaluation,* Chap. 7. Englewood Cliffs, N.J.: Prentice-Hall, Inc., 1975. Good analyses of the nature of criterion-referenced tests and the problems of constructing them.

2

Planning the Test

The key to effective achievement testing is careful planning. It provides greater assurance that our test will measure relevant learning outcomes. . . . measure a representative sample of the desired behaviors. . . . and provide dependable information on which to base instructional decisions. . . . Test planning involves the identification and specification of precisely what is to be measured.

The planning of an achievement test can take many forms, but both professional test makers and classroom teachers have found the following series of steps to be most useful.

1. Determine the purpose of the test.
2. Identify the learning outcomes to be measured by the test.
3. Define the learning outcomes in terms of specific, observable behavior.
4. Outline the subject matter to be measured by the test.
5. Prepare a table of specifications.
6. Use the table of specifications as a basis for preparing tests.

It is obvious from this list that the major consideration in test planning is to determine *what* is to be measured, and to describe it in such precise terms that test items can be constructed that call forth the desired behavior.

Determining the Purpose of the Test

As we noted in Chapter 1, tests can be used in an instructional program to assess entry behavior (placement test), monitor learning progress (formative test), diagnose learning difficulties (diagnostic test), and measure performance at the end of instruction (summative test). Each type of test use typically requires some modification in test design. Although the specific make-up of any test depends on the particular situation in which it is to be used, it is possible to identify some of the common characteristics of the various test types. These have been summarized in Table 2.1.

Table 2.1. *Characteristics of Four Types of Achievement Tests*

TYPE OF TEST	FUNCTION OF TEST	SAMPLING CONSIDERATIONS	ITEM CHARACTERISTICS
PLACEMENT	Measure prerequisite entry skills	Include each prerequisite entry behavior	Typically, items are easy and criterion-referenced
	Determine entry performance on course objectives	Select representative sample of course objectives	Typically, items have a wide range of difficulty and are norm-referenced
FORMATIVE	Provide feedback to students and teacher on learning progress	Include all unit objectives, if possible (or those most essential)	Items match difficulty of unit objectives and are criterion-referenced
DIAGNOSTIC	Determine causes of recurring learning difficulties	Include sample of tasks based on common sources of learning error	Typically, items are easy and are used to pinpoint specific causes of error
SUMMATIVE	Assign grades, or certify mastery, at end of instruction	Select representative sample of course objectives	Typically, items have a wide range of difficulty and are norm-referenced

Adapted from P. W. Airasian and G. F. Madaus, "Functional Types of Student Evaluation," *Measurement and Evaluation in Guidance,* 4 (1972), 221–33.

The material in Table 2.1 provides a good general description of the four basic test types we have discussed, but it must be recognized that the categories overlap to some degree. In some instances, a particular test may be designed to serve more than one function. For example, an end-of-unit formative test may be used to provide feedback to students, to pinpoint sources of learning error, and to certify mastery of the unit objectives. Similarly, sampling considerations and item characteristics may need to be modified to fit a particular test use or a specific type of instruction. Despite the lack of discrete categories, however, the table highlights the variety of functions that achievement tests can serve and some of the basic considerations in preparing each type of test. Thus, it serves as a good general framework for test planning.

Identifying the Intended Learning Outcomes

The learning outcomes measured by a test should faithfully reflect the objectives of instruction. Thus, the first order of business is to identify those instructional objectives that are to be measured by the test and then make certain that they are stated in a manner that is useful for testing. This is easier said than done. It is especially difficult if a clearly defined set of instructional objectives is not available to begin with, as is usually the case. One useful guide for approaching this task is the *Taxonomy of Educational Objectives* (see Bloom et al., 1956; Krathwohl et al., 1964; Harrow, 1972). This is a comprehensive system that classifies objectives within each of three domains: (1) cognitive, (2) affective, and (3) psychomotor. The cognitive domain of the taxonomy is concerned with intellectual outcomes, the affective domain with interests and attitudes, and the psychomotor domain with motor skills. Since our concern here is with achievement testing, we shall focus primarily on the cognitive domain.

COGNITIVE DOMAIN OF THE TAXONOMY

Intellectual outcomes in the cognitive domain are divided into two major classes: (1) knowledge and (2) intellectual abilities and skills. These are further subdivided into six main areas as follows:

Knowledge

1.00 KNOWLEDGE (Remembering previously learned material)
  1.10 Knowledge of specifics
    1.11 Knowledge of terms

1.12 Knowledge of specific facts
1.20 Knowledge of ways and means of dealing with specifics
1.21 Knowledge of conventions
1.22 Knowledge of trends and sequences
1.23 Knowledge of classifications and categories
1.24 Knowledge of criteria
1.25 Knowledge of methodology
1.30 Knowledge of the universals and abstractions in a field
1.31 Knowledge of principles and generalizations
1.32 Knowledge of theories and structures

Intellectual Abilities and Skills

2.00 COMPREHENSION (Grasping the meaning of material)
2.10 Translation (Converting from one form to another)
2.20 Interpretation (Explaining or summarizing material)
2.30 Extrapolation (Extending the meaning beyond the data)
3.00 APPLICATION (Using information in concrete situations)
4.00 ANALYSIS (Breaking down material into its parts)
4.10 Analysis of elements (Identifying the parts)
4.20 Analysis of relationships (Identifying the relationship)
4.30 Analysis of organizational principles (Identifying the way the parts are organized)
5.00 SYNTHESIS (Putting parts together into a whole)
5.10 Production of a unique communication
5.20 Production of a plan or proposed set of operations
5.30 Derivation of a set of abstract relations
6.00 EVALUATION (Judging the value of a thing for a given purpose using definite criteria)
6.10 Judgments in terms of internal evidence
6.20 Judgments in terms of external criteria[1]

As can be seen in this outline, the outcomes are arranged in order of increasing complexity. They begin with the relatively simple recall of factual information, proceed to the lowest level of understanding (comprehension), and then advance through the increasingly complex levels of application, analysis, synthesis, and evaluation. The subdivisions within each area are also listed in order of increasing complexity. This scheme for classifying student behavior is thus hierarchical. That is, the more complex behaviors include the simpler behaviors listed in the lower categories.

The cognitive domain of the taxonomy is especially useful in planning the achievement test. It focuses on a comprehensive and apparently complete list of mental processes to be considered when identifying

[1] Reprinted from Benjamin S. Bloom, ed., et al., *Taxonomy of Educational Objectives: Cognitive Domain* (New York: David McKay Co., Inc., 1956), pp. 201–7. Reprinted with permission of the publisher.

learning outcomes, it provides a standard vocabulary for describing and classifying learning outcomes, and it serves as a guide for stating learning outcomes in terms of specific student behaviors.

DETERMINING THE OUTCOMES TO BE TESTED

The instructional objectives for a particular course will depend on the specific nature of the course, the objectives attained in previous courses, the philosophy of the school, the special needs of the students, and a host of other local factors that have a bearing on the instructional program. Despite the variation from course to course, most lists of instructional objectives include learning outcomes in the following areas: (1) knowledge, (2) intellectual abilities and skills, (3) general skills (laboratory, performance, communication, work-study), and (4) attitudes, interests, and appreciations. It is in the first two areas, which are covered by the cognitive domain of the taxonomy, that achievement testing is most useful. Learning outcomes in the other areas are typically evaluated by rating scales, check lists, anecdotal records, inventories, and similar nontest evaluation procedures. Thus, the first step is to separate from the list of instructional objectives those that are testable by paper-and-pencil test. If the instructional objectives have not yet been determined, the cognitive domain of the taxonomy can be used as a frame of reference for determining them.

Although the cognitive domain of the taxonomy provides a valuable guide for identifying learning outcomes, not all of the areas listed under this domain will be covered in a particular test or even in a particular course. Moreover, the classification scheme is neutral concerning the relative importance of the learning outcomes listed. Thus, it is the instructor who must decide which learning outcomes will guide her teaching and testing, and how much emphasis each outcome will receive. The taxonomy serves merely as a convenient check list of outcomes that prevents relevant areas of student behavior from being overlooked during the planning of an achievement test.

In planning a *formative* test, Bloom, Hastings, and Madaus (1971) have found the following categories of student behavior especially useful:

knowledge of terms
knowledge of facts
knowledge of rules and principles
skill in using processes and procedures
ability to make translations
ability to make applications

Although the fourth category (skill) is not included in the cognitive domain of the taxonomy, Bloom et al. found that it appeared in many academic courses and could frequently be measured by paper-and-pencil test. The skill of computing a square root, for example, can easily be tested. Such skills involve the ability to use a process or procedure (that is, to follow the steps correctly) without necessarily understanding the principles involved.

In planning a *summative* test, all areas of the cognitive domain might have to be included. Whereas the formative test focuses on the specific outcomes of a limited segment of instruction, the summative test must be concerned with the integration of material from the various instructional units. Thus, the summative test can typically be expected to include some items that measure the higher abilities listed in the taxonomy—analysis, synthesis, and evaluation.

Planning a *placement* test of prerequisite skills includes identifying all entry behaviors that are necessary for success in a particular instructional unit or course. Similarly, planning a *diagnostic* test includes identifying the common sources of error in a particular unit or course. Thus, the make-up of these two test types is determined by the particular segment of instruction they are being designed for, and it is not possible to prespecify the types of learning tasks to be included. As we noted earlier, however, the items in both tests are typically easy and are confined to a rather limited set of tasks.

STATING THE GENERAL LEARNING OUTCOMES

The learning outcomes to be measured by a test are most useful in test planning when they are stated as *terminal* behavior that is *observable*. That is, they should indicate clearly the student performance to be demonstrated at the end of the learning experience. The following list of learning outcomes for a unit in the construction of achievement tests illustrates this type of statement. Note that these statements cover only those objectives that can be tested and that they are stated as *general outcomes*. Before being used for test planning, each statement would have to be defined further in terms of specific student behaviors.

At the end of this unit in achievement testing the student will demonstrate that he:

1. Knows the common terms used in achievement testing.
2. Knows the procedures for planning, constructing, and appraising achievement tests.
3. Knows the major categories of the cognitive domain of the taxonomy.

4. Knows the various types of test items and the advantages, limitations, and uses of each type.
5. Comprehends the principles of achievement testing.
6. Comprehends the concepts of validity and reliability and their role in the construction and use of achievement tests.
7. Comprehends how achievement testing can contribute to the teaching-learning process.
8. Identifies learning outcomes that are properly stated in behavioral terms.
9. Relates test items to the learning outcomes they measure.
10. Detects common errors in test items.
11. Interprets achievement-test scores, item-analysis data, and validity and reliability data.
12. Evaluates a complete achievement test, pointing out its strengths and weaknesses for a given purpose.

This list of outcomes illustrates the broad range of behaviors that can be measured by paper-and-pencil tests. The list could, of course, be expanded by making the statements more specific, or it could be condensed by combining the outcomes into more general statements. The number of statements is somewhat arbitrary: somewhere between eight and fifteen general learning outcomes provide a list that is both useful and manageable. It is also helpful to include only one learning outcome in each statement.

Defining the General Outcomes in Specific Terms

When a satisfactory list of general learning outcomes has been identified and clearly stated, the next step is to list the specific student behaviors that are to be accepted as evidence that the outcomes have been achieved. For example, what specific behaviors will show that a student "knows the common terms used in achievement testing" or "comprehends the principles of achievement testing?" Specific behaviors for these two areas may be listed as follows:

1. Knows common terms used in achievement testing
   - 1.1 Identifies the correct definitions of terms
   - 1.2 Identifies the meaning of terms when used in context
   - 1.3 Distinguishes between terms on basis of meaning
   - 1.4 Selects the most appropriate terms when describing testing procedures
5. Comprehends the principles of achievement testing
   - 5.1 Describes each principle in her own words
   - 5.2 Matches a specific example to each principle

5.3 Explains the relevance of each principle to the major steps in test construction
5.4 Predicts the most probable effect of violating each of the principles
5.5 Formulates a test plan that is in harmony with the principles

Note that the terms used to describe the specific learning outcomes indicate behaviors that can be demonstrated to an observer. That is, the outcomes are *observable* behaviors that can be called forth by test items. Here are the *specific behavioral terms* that were used to define the above learning outcomes:

Identifies	Matches
Distinguishes between	Explains
Selects	Predicts
Describes	Formulates

Action verbs such as these indicate precisely what the student must be able to do to demonstrate his achievement. Such vague and indefinite terms as "learns," "sees," "realizes," and "is familiar with" should be avoided, since they do not clearly indicate the terminal behavior to be observed.

Some sample action verbs for stating specific learning outcomes at each level of the cognitive domain of the taxonomy are presented in Table 2.2. Although some action verbs (for instance, "identifies") may

Table 2.2. *Illustrative Action Verbs for Defining Objectives in the Cognitive Domain of the Taxonomy*

TAXONOMY CATEGORIES	SAMPLE VERBS FOR STATING SPECIFIC LEARNING OUTCOMES
KNOWLEDGE	Identifies, names, defines, describes, lists, matches, selects, outlines
COMPREHENSION	Classifies, explains, summarizes, converts, predicts, distinguishes between
APPLICATION	Demonstrates, computes, solves, modifies, arranges, operates, relates
ANALYSIS	Differentiates, diagrams, estimates, separates, infers, orders, subdivides
SYNTHESIS	Combines, creates, formulates, designs, composes, constructs, rearranges, revises
EVALUATION	Judges, criticizes, compares, justifies, concludes, discriminates, supports

be used at different levels, this table provides a useful guide for defining intended outcomes in behavioral terms. For more comprehensive lists of action verbs, see Gronlund, 1970, 1976.

In defining the general learning outcomes in specific terms, it is frequently impossible to list all of the relevant behaviors. The proportion that need be listed depends to a large extent on the nature of the test. In planning a test that is used to *describe* which learning tasks a student has mastered (a criterion-referenced test), we should include as comprehensive a list of behaviors as possible. For a test that is used to *rank* students in order of achievement (a norm-referenced test), however, it is usually satisfactory to include enough behaviors to characterize the typical student who has achieved the outcomes.

Outlining the Subject Matter

The learning outcomes specify how students are expected to react to the subject matter of a course. Although it is possible to include both the student behavior and the specific subject matter the student is to behave toward in the same statement, it is usually desirable to list them separately. The reason for this is that the student can react in the same way to many different areas of subject matter, and he can react in many different ways to the same area of subject matter. For example, when we state that a student can "define a term in his own words," "recall a specific fact," or "give an example of a principle," these behaviors can be applied to almost any area of subject matter. Similarly, in studying the taxonomy of educational objectives we may expect students merely to recall the categories in it, or we could require them to explain the principles according to which it is organized, to summarize its usefulness in test planning, to classify a given set of learning outcomes with it, or to use it in the actual construction of a test. Since student behaviors can overlap a variety of subject-matter areas, and vice versa, it is more convenient to list each behavior and subject-matter area separately and then relate them in the table of specifications.

The content of a course may be outlined in detail for teaching purposes, but only the major categories need be listed in a test plan. The following outline of subject-matter topics covered in the first two chapters of this book are sufficiently detailed for a test plan.

A. Role of testing in the instructional process
   1. Instructional decisions and test types
   2. Influence of tests on learning and instruction
B. Principles of achievement testing

1. Relation to instructional objectives
2. Representative sampling
3. Relevance of items to outcomes
4. Relevance of test to use of results
5. Reliability of results
6. Improvement of learning
7. Norm-referenced versus criterion-referenced testing

C. Planning the test
1. Identifying learning outcomes
   a. Taxonomy: cognitive domain
   b. Determining outcomes for testing
   c. Stating the general learning outcomes
2. Defining the general outcomes in specific terms
3. Outlining the subject matter
4. Preparing a table of specifications
5. Using the table in test preparation

If a test were being planned to cover all of the chapters in this book, it might be necessary to include only the major headings (A, B, and C) in order to prevent the outline of content from becoming unmanageable.

Using the topics in this book as examples is not to imply that the content outline should be limited to the material in a particular book. An achievement test is typically designed to measure all of the course content, including that covered in class discussion, outside reading, and any other special assignments. Our example here is meant to illustrate the approximate amount of detail and not the source of the topics to be included.

Preparing a Table of Specifications

When the learning outcomes have been defined and the course content outlined, a table of specifications should be prepared. This is a table that relates outcomes to content and indicates the relative weight to be given to each of the various areas. As we noted earlier, the purpose of the table is to provide assurance that the test will measure a representative sample of the learning outcomes and the subject-matter topics to be measured.

An example of a table of specifications for a summative test (norm-referenced) on the first two chapters of this book is given in Table 2.3. Note that only the general learning outcomes relevant to these chapters and only the major subject-matter categories have been included. A more detailed table may be desirable for some test purposes, but the present table is sufficient for illustration.

The numbers in each cell of Table 2.3 indicate the number of test items to be devoted to that particular area. For example, ten items in the

Table 2.3. *Table of Specifications for a Summative Test on Chapters 1 and 2 of this Book*

OUTCOMES \ CONTENT	ROLE OF TESTS IN TEACHING	PRINCIPLES OF TESTING	PLANNING THE TEST	TOTAL NUMBER OF ITEMS
Knows terms	4	3	3	10
Knows procedures		3	7	10
Knows taxonomy categories			10	10
Comprehends principles	3	10	7	20
Comprehends applications in teaching	3	4	13	20
Identifies properly stated outcomes			10	10
Total number of items	10	20	50	80 items

test will measure knowledge of terms: four of them pertain to the "role of tests in teaching," three to "principles of testing," and three to "planning the test." The number of items assigned to each cell is determined by the weight given to each learning outcome and each subject-matter area.

A number of factors influence the assigning of relative weights to each learning outcome and each content area. For example, how important is each area in the total learning experience? How much time was devoted to each area during instruction? Which outcomes have the greatest retention and transfer value? What relative importance do curriculum specialists assign to each area? These and similar criteria must be considered in determining the relative importance of each outcome and subject-matter area. In the final analysis, however, the weights assigned to the outcomes and topics listed in the table should faithfully reflect the emphasis given during instruction. In Table 2.3, for example, it is assumed that much more emphasis was given to planning the test (50 items) than was given to the other two content areas. Similarly, it is assumed that knowledge outcomes (30 items) were given more than one third of the emphasis during instruction and that comprehension outcomes (40 items) were given approximately half of the total emphasis.

In summary, the preparation of a table of specifications includes the following steps:

1. Identify the learning outcomes and content areas to be measured by the test.
2. Weight these outcomes and topics according to their relative importance.
3. Build the table in accordance with these relative weights by distributing the test items proportionately among the cells of the table.

The resulting two-way table indicates the type of test needed to measure the learning outcomes and course content in a balanced manner.

A formative test (criterion-referenced) typically covers such a limited segment of instruction that all specific learning outcomes and all important subject-matter topics might be included in the table of specifications. In some cases, the test may cover such a limited area that a table of specifications is unnecessary. In constructing a formative test on "knowledge of the cognitive domain of the taxonomy," for example, a list of the specific ways students are to demonstrate their knowledge (listing categories in order, identifying examples of categories, and so on) may be sufficient for test planning. Since formative tests are used to identify the specific tasks students can and cannot perform, a more detailed test plan is typically required for this type of test than for a summative test (norm-referenced).

Using the Table of Specifications in Test Preparation

The table of specifications is like a blueprint to the test maker. It specifies the number and the nature of the items in the test, thereby providing a guide for item writing. If the table has been carefully prepared and the learning outcomes clearly specified, the quality of the test will depend largely on how closely the test maker can match the specifications.

MATCHING ITEMS TO SPECIFIC LEARNING OUTCOMES

The key to effective achievement testing is to construct a set of test items that call forth the behavior described in the intended learning outcomes. Although we can never be certain of a perfect correspondence, we will do well to follow the examples below, which illustrate how test items should be written in order to measure the behavior stated in the specific learning outcomes.

Examples

Specific Learning Outcome: Defines terms in his own words.

Directions: Define each of the following terms in a sentence or two.

1. Taxonomy.
2. Cognitive.
3. Measurement.
4. Evaluation.

Specific Learning Outcome: Identifies procedural steps in planning a test.

1. Which one of the following steps should be completed first in planning an achievement test?[2]
   A. Select the types of test items to use.
   B. Decide on the length of the test.
   *C. Define the instructional objectives.
   D. Build a table of specifications.

Specific Learning Outcome: Identifies the hierarchical order of the categories in the cognitive domain of the taxonomy.

1. Which one of the following categories in the taxonomy indicates the highest level of learning?
   A. Analysis.
   B. Application.
   C. Comprehension.
   *D. Synthesis.

Specific Learning Outcome: Distinguishes between sound and unsound principles of achievement testing.

Directions: Read each of the following statements. If the statement indicates a sound principle of achievement testing, circle the S; if it indicates an unsound principle, circle the U.

*S U 1. The specific learning outcomes to be tested should be stated in terms of student behavior.

S *U 2. Achievement testing should be limited to outcomes that can be measured objectively.

*S U 3. Each achievement-test item should measure a clearly defined subject-matter topic and a clearly defined student behavior.

Specific Learning Outcome: Identifies examples of properly stated learning outcomes.

1. Which one of the following learning outcomes is properly stated in behavioral terms?
   A. Student realizes the importance of tests in teaching.

[2] Throughout this book, the correct answer is indicated by an asterisk.

B. Student has acquired the basic principles of achievement testing.
C. Student demonstrates a desire for more experience in test construction.
*D. Student predicts the most probable effect of violating a test-construction principle.

Note in these examples that each specific learning outcome provides a precise definition of the student behavior to be observed, and that the test item simply provides a task that makes observation of the specified behavior possible.

TEST LENGTH

The length of a test is determined at the same time that the table of specifications is prepared. Although test length is influenced by a host of factors (such as purpose of test, type of test items, age of students, and time available for testing), a basic consideration in effective testing is the number of test items devoted to each instructional objective. We need a large enough number to provide an adequate sample of the learning tasks encompassed by each objective. As a general guide, it is usually desirable to include at least several objective test items for each specific learning outcome to be measured and ten or more items for each general objective.

ITEM DIFFICULTY

Decisions concerning item difficulty are guided to a large extent by the nature of the achievement test being prepared. If the test is to be criterion-referenced, item difficulty is determined by the difficulty of the learning tasks described in the specific learning outcomes. If the test is to be norm-referenced, item difficulty is deliberately altered in order that a wide spread of test scores may be obtained. These different approaches to item difficulty constitute one of the major distinctions between criterion-referenced and norm-referenced testing.

Since a criterion-referenced test is designed to describe the specific learning tasks an individual can and cannot perform, item difficulty should match the difficulty of the task. If the task is easy, the test items should be easy. If the task is difficult, the test items should be difficult. No item should be eliminated simply because most students might be expected to answer it correctly, or because it might be answered incorrectly by most students. Likewise, no attempt should be made to alter item difficulty in order to obtain a spread of test scores. What we seek in a criterion-referenced test is a set of test items that can be used to describe how well a student performs on a clearly defined domain of learning tasks, without reference to the performance of others. To serve this function effectively, the test items must match the learning tasks as closely as possible in all respects, including item difficulty.

Norm-referenced achievement tests are designed to rank individuals in order of their achievement. For this purpose, and in order that a reliable ranking may be obtained, a wide spread of test scores is needed. For example, we can say with greater confidence that Mary has achieved more than Tom if the difference in test scores is ten points rather than two. Thus, the ability of test items to discriminate among students is vital to norm-referenced testing, and, typically, the greater the spread of scores the better.

The desired score variability in norm-referenced tests is obtained by eliminating the very easy items (those likely to be answered correctly by all students) and by constructing the majority of items at an average level of difficulty—that is, a level at which approximately half of the students answer correctly. Although some easy items may be desirable at the beginning of the test for motivational purposes, and some difficult ones at the end to challenge the high achievers, items of average difficulty should be favored because they provide for maximum discrimination among individuals. Item difficulty and item discrimination will be described in greater detail in the discussion of item analysis in Chapter 7.

In deliberately altering item difficulty in norm-referenced testing in order to provide for the desired spread of scores, take care to keep the items relevant to the learning outcomes to be measured. In measuring the ability to distinguish between concepts, for example, item difficulty can be increased by calling for finer discriminations. Similarly, in measuring the ability to apply principles to new situations, items can be constructed that call for increasingly complex applications. Item difficulty should not be increased by measuring more obscure material, or by overloading the test with items on a particular learning outcome that happens to be difficult. Although a norm-referenced achievement test is designed to rank students from high to low, that ranking should represent the relative degree to which the instructional objectives are being achieved.

Other Considerations in Test Planning

In this chapter, we have emphasized those aspects of test planning that are concerned with the preparation of an achievement test that measures a balanced sample of clearly defined learning outcomes. A complete test plan will, of course, also consider such things as test directions, arrangement of the items in the test, scoring, and whether to correct for guessing. These and similar factors will be discussed in Chapter 7. In the intervening chapters we will describe the procedures for constructing the various types of items used in achievement tests.

Additional Reading

BLOOM, B. S., ed., et al., *Taxonomy of Educational Objectives: Cognitive Domain.* New York: David McKay Co., Inc., 1956. Describes and illustrates the categories in the cognitive domain.

BLOOM, B. S., J. T. HASTINGS, and G. F. MADAUS, *Handbook on Formative and Summative Evaluation of Student Learning,* Chap. 2. New York: McGraw-Hill Book Company, 1971. Extended discussion of defining educational objectives.

GRONLUND, N. E., *Stating Behavioral Objectives for Classroom Instruction.* New York: Macmillan Publishing Co., Inc., 1970. Brief how-to-do-it book (58 pages) on preparing instructional objectives.

———, *Measurement and Evaluation in Teaching* (3rd ed.), Chaps. 2, 3, and 6. New York: Macmillan Publishing Co., Inc., 1976. Comprehensive treatment of instructional objectives and their role in planning the classroom test.

HARROW, A. J., *A Taxonomy of the Psychomotor Domain.* New York: David McKay Co., Inc., 1972. Describes and illustrates a set of categories in the psychomotor domain.

KRATHWOHL, D. R., B. S. BLOOM, and B. B. MASIA, *Taxonomy of Educational Objectives: Affective Domain.* New York: David McKay Co., Inc., 1964. Describes and illustrates the categories in the affective domain.

KRATHWOHL, D. R., and D. A. PAYNE, "The Nature and Definition of Educational Objectives and Strategies for their Assessment," in *Educational Measurement* (2nd ed.), ed. R. L. Thorndike, Chap. 2. Washington, D.C.: American Council on Education, 1971. Comprehensive treatment of objectives and their use in testing and evaluation.

TINKLEMAN, S. N., "Planning the Objective Test," *Educational Measurement* (2nd ed.), ed. R. L. Thorndike, Chap. 3. Washington, D.C.: American Council on Education, 1971. Detailed descriptions of the steps in test planning.

3

Constructing Objective Tests of Knowledge

Objective test items can be used to measure a variety of knowledge outcomes. . . . The most generally useful is the multiple-choice item . . . but other item types also have a place. . . . Following simple but important rules for construction can improve the quality of objective test items.

In the last chapter, we stressed the importance of clearly defining the learning outcomes to be measured, of preparing a table of specifications, and of constructing test items that measure each learning outcome as directly as possible. These steps are necessary if we want an achievement test to provide a sample of student behavior that is both relevant to and representative of the instructional objectives of the course.

In constructing an achievement test to fit a table of specifications, the test maker may choose from a variety of item types. Some of the item types are referred to as *objective* items, because they can be scored objectively. That is, equally competent scorers can score them independently and obtain the same results. Objective test items include the following selection-type items: multiple-choice, true-false, and matching. They also include the supply-type items that are limited to short answers (several words or less), even though such items are not completely objective. The other supply-type item, the essay question, is subjective. That is, the subjective judgment of the scorer enters into the scoring, and, thus, the scores differ from one scorer to another, and from one time to another for the same scorer.

Knowledge[1] outcomes are typically measured by objective test items because these item types (1) can be adapted more easily to the specific learning outcomes to be measured, (2) provide for more adequate sampling of student behavior, and (3) as we noted above, can be scored more quickly and objectively. Essay questions are generally reserved for measuring the more complex learning outcomes, where the difficulties in scoring are offset by the importance of the outcomes and by the unique responses that can be called forth by such questions (the ability to create, the ability to organize, and so on).

Selecting the Type of Objective Test Item to Use

There are two major considerations in selecting the specific type of test item to use. The first is the nature of the learning outcome. As we noted earlier, a test item should measure the learning outcome as directly as possible, and this frequently dictates a specific item type. The second consideration is the quality of the item that can be constructed. Other things being equal, multiple-choice items tend to provide the highest-quality items. That is, when the various test items are equally adaptable to the learning outcomes and subject matter to be measured, multiple-choice items will generally provide a more adequate measure than the other item types. Add to this the fact that multiple-choice items can measure a variety of learning outcomes, ranging from simple to complex, and it is easy to see why this item type is regarded so highly and used so widely.

An effective test-construction procedure, one that takes into account both of the above considerations, is to start each item as a multiple-choice item, switching to another item type only when the learning outcome or subject matter makes it desirable to do so. Thus, when there are only two possible alternatives a shift can be made to a true-false item, when there are a number of similar factors to be related a shift can be made to a matching item, and when the ability to supply the answer is a significant element a shift can be made to a short-answer item.

The multiple-choice item plays such an important role in the objective testing of knowledge outcomes that it will be treated first and in considerable detail. This presentation will be followed by a briefer dis-

[1] *Knowledge,* as used in this chapter, is defined as in the Taxonomy of Educational Objectives (Bloom et al., 1956): the simple remembering of previously learned material. (See the outline of the cognitive domain of the Taxonomy in Chapter 2.)

cussion of each of the other types of objective items: true-false, matching, and short-answer.

Constructing Multiple–Choice Items

The multiple-choice item consists of a *stem,* which presents a problem situation, and several *alternatives,* which provide possible solutions to the problem. The stem may be a question or an incomplete statement. The alternatives include the correct answer and several plausible wrong answers, called *distracters.* The function of the latter is to distract those students who are uncertain of the answer.

The following items illustrate the question form and the incomplete-statement form of a multiple-choice item.

Which one of the following item types is an example of a supply-type test item?
A. Multiple-choice item.
B. True-false item.
C. Matching item.
*D. Short-answer item.

An example of a supply-type test item is the:
A. multiple-choice item.
B. true-false item.
C. matching item.
*D. short-answer item.

Note in these examples that both stems pose the same problem, but that the incomplete statement is more concise. This is typically the case. The question form is easier to write and forces the test maker to pose a clear problem but tends to result in a longer stem. An effective procedure for the beginner is to start with a question and shift to the incomplete statement only if greater conciseness can be obtained by doing so.

The alternatives in the above examples contain only one correct answer, and the distracters are clearly incorrect. Another type of multiple-choice item is the *best-answer* form, in which the alternatives are all partially correct but one is clearly better than the others. This type is used for more complex achievement, as when the student must select the best reason for an action, the best method for doing something, or the best application of a principle. Thus, whether the correct-answer or best-answer form is used depends on the learning outcomes to be measured. Since any given test is likely to contain items of both types, it is important that the directions tell the student to select the *best* answer.

The above examples also illustrate the use of four alternatives. Multiple-choice items typically include either four or five choices. The larger number will, of course, reduce the student's chances of obtaining the correct answer by guessing. Theoretically, with five alternatives he has only one chance in five of guessing the answer, whereas with four alternatives he has one chance in four. It is frequently difficult for the instructor to present five plausible choices, however, and an item is not improved by adding an obviously wrong answer merely to obtain five alternatives. There is no reason why the items in a given test should all have the same number of alternatives. Some might contain four and some five, depending on the availability of plausible distracters. This would pose a problem only if the test were to be corrected for guessing, a practice, as we shall see later, that is not recommended for classroom achievement tests.

USES OF MULTIPLE-CHOICE ITEMS

The multiple-choice item can be used to measure both knowledge outcomes and various types of intellectual skills. Its use in measuring the more complex learning outcomes will be considered in the next chapter. Here, we shall confine our discussion to the measurement of knowledge outcomes—specifically, those included in the cognitive domain of the Taxonomy of Educational Objectives (Bloom et al, 1956).

The wide applicability of the multiple-choice item can probably be shown best by illustrating some of the types of questions that can be asked in each of the knowledge areas. Only the portion of each question that is applicable to a variety of content areas has been included. The beginner in test construction may find these examples of different types of questions useful in preparing multiple-choice items in the knowledge area.

1.11 Knowledge of Terminology

What word means the same as ________?
Which statement best defines the term ________?
In the following context, what is the meaning of the word ________?
What is (some process) called?

1.12 Knowledge of Specific Facts

Where would you find ________?
In what year did ________?
Who first discovered ________?
What is the name of ________?
What is the most important characteristic of ________?
What is the main difference between ________?

1.21 Knowledge of Conventions

What is the correct form for ________?
Which one of the following symbols is used for ________?
Which statement indicates correct usage of ________?
Which one of the following rules applies to ________?

Which one of the following methods is most commonly used to ________?

1.22 Knowledge of Trends and Sequences

Which one of the following best describes the present trend of ________?
What is the most important cause of ________?
What will be the effect of ________?
What would be the shape of the curve for ________?
Which one of the following sequences indicates the proper order of ________?

1.23 Knowledge of Classification and Categories

What are the main types of ________?
What are the major classifications of ________?
What are the characteristics of ________?
How would you classify ________?
Which one of the following is an example of ________?

1.24 Knowledge of Criteria

Which one of the following is a criterion for judging ________?
What criteria were used by ________ to judge ________?
What is the most important criterion for selecting ________?
What criteria are used to classify ________?
Which one of the following is *not* an important criterion for ________?

1.25 Knowledge of Methodology

What method is used for ________?
What is the best way to ________?
What would be the first step in making ________?
What is the most important difference between the ________ and the ________ method?
Which one of the following would be essential in making ________?
What would be the minimum equipment needed to ________?

1.31 Knowledge of Principles and Generalizations

Which statement best expresses the principle of ________?
Which statement best summarizes the belief that ________?
Which one of the following principles best explains ________?
Which one of the following principles is most useful in predicting ________?
Which one of the following illustrates the principle of ________?

1.32 Knowledge of Theories and Structures

Which statement is most consistent with the theory of ________?
Which principles are essential to the theory of ________?
Which one of the following is the most complete formulation of ________?
Which one of the following best describes the structure and organization of ________?
What evidence best supports the theory of ________?

The above questions, of course, provide only a sample of the many questions that could be asked in each knowledge area. Also, the questions are of necessity stated in rather general terms. Stems for multiple-choice items in specific subjects would tend to use language that is related more directly to the particular topic. In many instances, it may also be desirable to shift to the incomplete-statement form, for greater clarity and conciseness. Thus, these questions are best viewed as examples of the variety of problem situations that multiple-choice items can present in each of the various knowledge areas.

RULES FOR CONSTRUCTING MULTIPLE-CHOICE ITEMS

Ideally, a multiple-choice item presents students with a task that is both important and clearly understood, and one that can be answered correctly only by those who have achieved the desired learning. The following rules for construction are intended as guides for the preparation of items that approximate this ideal.

1. Design each item to measure an important learning outcome. The problem situation around which an item is to be built should be important and should be directly related to the learning outcomes (objectives) of the course. Avoid testing for unimportant details, unrelated bits of information, and material that is irrelevant to the desired outcomes. The questions in the previous section illustrate some of the more fundamental aspects of knowledge that might be measured. In testing for these knowledge outcomes, however, focus on the more important terms, facts, and principles. Resist the temptation to increase item difficulty by resorting to the more obscure and less significant items of knowledge. Remember that each test item is expected to call forth student behavior that will help determine the extent to which the instructional objectives of the course have been achieved.

2. Present a single clearly formulated problem in the stem of the item. The task set forth in the stem of the item should be so clear that a student can understand it without reading the alternatives. In fact, a good check on the clarity and completeness of a multiple-choice stem is to cover the alternatives and determine whether it could be answered without the choices. Try this on the two sample items that follow.

Example

Poor: A table of specifications:
- A. indicates how a test will be used to improve learning.
- *B. provides a more balanced sampling of content.
- C. arranges the instructional objectives in order of their importance.
- D. specifies the method of scoring to be used on a test.

Better: What is the main advantage of using a table of specifications when preparing an achievement test?

A. It reduces the amount of time required.
*B. It improves the sampling of content.
C. It makes the construction of test items easier.
D. It increases the objectivity of the test.

The first of these examples is no more than a collection of true-false statements with a common stem. The problem presented in the stem of the improved version is clear enough to serve as a supply-type short-answer item. The alternatives simply provide a series of possible answers from which to choose.

Note also in the second version that a *single* problem is presented in the stem. Including more than one problem usually adds to the complexity of the wording and reduces the diagnostic value of the item. When a student fails such an item, there is no way to determine which of the problems prevented her from responding correctly.

3. State the stem of the item in simple, clear language. The problem in the stem of a multiple-choice item should be stated as precisely as possible and should be free of unnecessarily complex wording and sentence structure. Anyone who possesses the knowledge measured by a test item should be able to select the correct answer. Poorly stated item stems frequently introduce sufficient ambiguity to prevent a knowledgeable student from responding correctly. Also, complex sentence structure may make the item a measure more of reading comprehension than of the intended knowledge outcome. The first of the two examples that follow is an extreme instance of this problem.

Example

Poor: The paucity of plausible, but incorrect, statements that can be related to a central idea poses a problem when constructing which one of the following types of test items?
A. Short-answer.
B. True-false.
*C. Multiple-choice.
D. Essay.

Better: The lack of plausible, but incorrect, alternatives will cause the greatest difficulty when constructing:
A. short-answer items.
B. true-false items.
*C. multiple-choice items.
D. essay items.

Another common fault in stating multiple-choice items is to load the stem with irrelevant and, thus, nonfunctioning material. This is probably caused by the instructor's desire to continue to teach his students—even while testing them. The following example illustrates the use of an item stem as "another chance to inform students."

Example

Poor: Testing can contribute to the instructional program of the school in many important ways. However, the main function of testing in teaching is:

Better: The main function of testing in teaching is:

The first version increases reading time and makes no contribution to the measurement of the specific knowledge outcome. Time spent in reading such irrelevant material could be spent more profitably in thinking about the problem presented. But if the purpose of an item is to measure a student's ability to distinguish between relevant and irrelevant material, this rule must, of course, be disregarded.

4. Put as much of the wording as possible in the stem of the item. Avoid repeating the same material in each of the alternatives. By moving all of the common content to the stem, it is usually possible to clarify the problem further and to reduce the time the student needs to read the alternatives. Note the improvement in the following item when this rule is followed.

Example

Poor: In *objective* testing, the term *objective:*

A. refers to the method of identifying the learning outcomes.
B. refers to the method of selecting the test content.
C. refers to the method of presenting the problem.
*D. refers to the method of scoring the answers.

Better: In *objective* testing, the term *objective* refers to the method of:

A. identifying the learning outcomes.
B. selecting the test content.
C. presenting the problem.
*D. scoring the answers.

In many cases, the problem is not simply to move the common words to the stem, but to reword the entire item. The following examples illustrates how an item can be improved by revising the stem and shortening the alternatives.

Example

Poor: Instructional objectives are most apt to be useful for test-construction purposes when they are stated in such a way that they show:

A. the course content to be covered during the instructional period.
*B. the kinds of behavior students should demonstrate upon reaching the goal.
C. the things the teacher will do to obtain maximum student learning.
D. the types of learning activities to be participated in during the course.

Better: Instructional objectives are most useful for test-construction purposes when they are stated in terms of:

A. course content.
*B. student behavior.
C. teacher behavior.
D. learning activities.

It is, of course, impossible to streamline all items in this manner, but economy of wording and clarity of expression are important goals to strive for in test construction.

5. State the stem of the item in positive form, wherever possible. A positively phrased test item tends to measure more important learning outcomes than a negatively stated item. This is because knowing such things as the *best* method or the *most relevant* argument typically has greater educational significance than knowing the *poorest* method or the *least relevant* argument. The use of negatively stated item stems results all too frequently from the ease with which such items can be constructed, rather than from the importance of the learning outcomes measured. The test maker who becomes frustrated by her inability to think of a sufficient number of plausible distracters for an item, as in the first example below, suddenly realizes how simple it would be to construct the second version.

Example

Item one: Which one of the following is a category in the taxonomy of the cognitive domain?

*A. Comprehension.
B. (*distracter needed*)
C. (*distracter needed*)
D. (*distracter needed*)

Item two: Which one of the following is *not* a category in the taxonomy of the cognitive domain?
A. Comprehension.
B. Application.
C. Analysis.
*D. (*answer needed*)

Note in the second version that the categories of the taxonomy serve as distracters and that all that is needed to complete the item is a correct answer. This could be any term that appears plausible but is *not* one of the categories listed in the taxonomy. Although such items are easily constructed, they are apt to have a low level of difficulty and are likely to measure relatively unimportant learning outcomes. Being able to identify answers that do *not* apply provides no assurance that the student possesses the desired knowledge.

The above solution to the lack of sufficient distracters is most likely to occur when the test maker is committed to the use of multiple-choice items only. A more desirable procedure for measuring the "ability to recognize the categories in the taxonomy of the cognitive domain" is to switch to a modified true-false form, as in the following example.

Example

Directions: Indicate which of the following are categories in the taxonomy of the cognitive domain, by circling Y for *yes* and N for *no.*
*Y N Comprehension.
Y N* Critical thinking.
Y N* Reasoning.
*Y N Synthesis.

In responding to this item, the student must make a separate judgment for each statement—the statement either is, or is not, one of the categories. Thus, the item calls for the type of behavior stated in the learning outcome, yet it avoids the problems of an insufficient number of distracters and of negative phrasing. This is a good illustration of the procedure discussed earlier—that is, starting with multiple-choice items and switching to other item types when more effective measurement requires it.

6. Emphasize negative wording whenever it is used in the stem of an item. In some instances the use of negative wording is basic to the measurement of an important learning outcome. Knowing that you should *not* cross the street against a red light or should *not* mix certain chemicals, for example, is so important that these precepts might be directly taught and directly tested. Any potentially dangerous situation may require a negative emphasis. There are also, of course, less dire circumstances where negative phrasing is useful. Almost any set of rules or procedures places some emphasis on practices to be avoided.

When negative wording is used in the stem of an item, it should be emphasized by being underlined or capitalized and by being placed near the end of the statement:

Example

Poor: Which one of the following is not a desirable practice when preparing multiple-choice items?
- A. Stating the stem in positive form.
- B. Using a stem that could function as a short-answer item.
- C. Underlining certain words in the stem for emphasis.
- *D. Shortening the stem by lengthening the alternatives.

Better: All of the following are desirable practices when preparing multiple-choice items EXCEPT:
- A. stating the stem in positive form.
- B. using a stem that could function as a short-answer item.
- C. underlining certain words in the stem for emphasis.
- *D. shortening the stem by lengthening the alternatives.

The improved version of this item assures that the item's negative aspect will not be overlooked, and it furnishes the student with the proper mind-set just before he reads the alternatives.

7. Make certain that the intended answer is correct or clearly best. When the correct-answer form of multiple-choice item is used, there should be only one correct answer and it should be unquestionably correct. With the best-answer form, the intended answer should be one that competent authorities would agree is clearly the best. In the latter case, it may also be necessary to include "of the following" in the stem of the item to allow for equally satisfactory answers that have not been included in the item:

Example

Poor: What is the best method of selecting course content for test items?

Better: Which one of the following is the best method of selecting course content for test items?

The proper phrasing of the stem of an item can also help avoid equivocal answers when the correct-answer form is used. In fact, an inadequately stated problem frequently makes the intended answer only partially correct or makes more than one alternative suitable:

Example

Poor: What is the purpose of classroom testing?

Better: One purpose of classroom testing is:

(or)

The main purpose of classroom testing is:

It is, of course, also necessary to check each of the distracters in the item to make certain that none of them could be defended as the correct answer. This will not only improve the quality of the item, but will also prevent a disruptive argument during the discussion of the test results.

8. Make all alternatives grammatically consistent with the stem of the item and parallel in form. The correct answer is usually carefully phrased so that it is grammatically consistent with the stem. Where the test maker is apt to slip is in stating the distracters. Unless care is taken to check them against the wording in the stem and in the correct answer, they may be inconsistent in tense, article, or grammatical form. This, of course, could provide a clue to the correct answer, or at least make some of the distracters ineffective.

A general step that can be taken to prevent grammatical inconsistency is to avoid using the articles "a" or "an" at the end of the stem of the item:

Example

Poor: The recall of factual information can be measured best with a:

A. matching item.
B. multiple-choice item.
*C. short-answer item.
D. essay question.

Better: The recall of factual information can be measured best with:

A. matching items.
B. multiple-choice items.
*C. short-answer items.
D. essay questions.

The indefinite article "a" in the first version makes the last distracter obviously wrong. By simply changing the alternatives from singular to plural, it is possible to omit the article. In other cases, it may be necessary to add an article ("a" or "an," as appropriate) to each alternative or to rephrase the entire item.

Stating all of the alternatives in parallel form also tends to prevent unnecessary clues from being given to the students. When the grammatical structure of one alternative differs from that of the others, some students may more readily detect that alternative as a correct or an incorrect response:

Example

Poor: Why should negative terms be avoided in the stem of a multiple-choice item?
*A. They may be overlooked.
B. The stem tends to be longer.
C. The construction of alternatives is more difficult.
D. The scoring is more difficult.

Better: Why should negative terms be avoided in the stem of a multiple-choice item?
*A. They may be overlooked.
B. They tend to increase the length of the stem.
C. They make the construction of alternatives more difficult.
D. They may increase the difficulty of the scoring.

In the first version, some students who lack the knowledge called for are apt to select the correct answer because of the way it is stated. The parallel grammatical structure in the second version removes this clue.

9. Avoid verbal clues that might enable students to select the correct answer or to eliminate an incorrect alternative. One of the most common sources of extraneous clues in multiple-choice items is the wording of the item. Some such clues are rather obvious and are easily avoided. Others require the constant attention of the test maker to prevent them from slipping in unnoticed. Let's review some of the verbal clues commonly found in multiple-choice items.

(a) *Similarity of wording in both the stem and the correct answer* is one of the more obvious clues. Key words in the stem may unintentionally be repeated verbatim in the correct answer, a synonym may be used, or the words may simply sound or look alike:

Example

Poor: Which one of the following would you consult first to locate research articles on achievement testing?

A. *Journal of Educational Psychology*
B. *Journal of Educational Measurement*
C. *Journal of Consulting Psychology*
*D. *Review of Educational Research*

The word "research" in both the stem and the correct answer is apt to provide a clue to the correct answer to the uninformed but testwise student. Such obvious clues might better be used in both the stem and an *incorrect* answer, in order to lead the uninformed *away* from the correct answer.

(b) *Stating the correct answer in textbook language or stereotyped phraseology* may cause the student to select it because it looks better than the other alternatives, or because he vaguely recalls having seen it before:

Example

Poor: Learning outcomes are most useful in preparing tests when they are:

*A. clearly stated in behavioral terms.
B. developed cooperatively by teachers and students.
C. prepared after the instruction has ended.
D. stated in general terms.

The pat phrasing of the correct answer is likely to give it away. Even the most poorly prepared student is apt to recognize the often repeated phrase "clearly stated in behavioral terms," although he might not have the foggiest notion of what it means.

(c) *Stating the correct answer in greater detail* may provide a clue. Also, when the answer is qualified by modifiers that are typically associated with true statements (for example, "sometimes," "may," "usually"), it is more likely to be chosen:

Example

Poor: Lack of attention to learning outcomes during test preparation:

A. will lower the technical quality of the items.
B. will make the construction of test items more difficult.

C. will result in the greater use of essay questions.
*D. may result in a test that is less relevant to the instructional program.

The term "may" is rather obvious in this example, but this type of error is common and appears frequently in a subtler form.

(d) *Including absolute terms in the distracters* enables students to eliminate them as possible answers, because such terms ("always," "never," "all," "none," "only," and so on) are commonly associated with false statements. This makes the correct answer obvious, or at least increases the chances that the students will guess it:

Example

Poor: Achievement tests help students improve their learning by:
A. encouraging them all to study hard.
*B. informing them of their progress.
C. giving them all a feeling of success.
D. preventing any of them from neglecting their assignments.

Such absolutes tend to be used by the inexperienced test maker to assure that the incorrect alternatives are clearly wrong. Unfortunately, they are easily recognized by the student as unlikely answers, making them ineffective as distracters.

(e) *Including two responses that are all-inclusive* makes it possible to eliminate the other alternatives, since one of the two must obviously be the correct answer:

Example

Poor: Which one of the following types of test items measures learning outcomes at the recall level?
*A. Supply-type items.
B. Selection-type items.
C. Matching items.
D. Multiple-choice items.

Since the first two alternatives include the only two major types of test items, even the poorly prepared student is likely to limit her choice to these two. This, of course, gives her a fifty-fifty chance of guessing the correct answer.

(f) *Including two responses that have the same meaning* makes it possible to eliminate them as potential answers. If two alternatives have the same meaning and only one answer is to be selected, it is fairly obvious that both alternatives must be incorrect:

Example

Poor: Which one of the following is the most important characteristic of achievement-test results?

A. Consistency.
B. Reliability.
*C. Relevance.
D. Objectivity.

In this item, both "consistency" and "reliability" can be eliminated because they mean essentially the same thing.

Extraneous clues to the correct answer must be excluded from test items if the items are to function as intended. It is frequently good practice, however, to use such clues to lead the uninformed away from the correct answer. If not overdone, this can contribute to the plausibility of the incorrect alternatives.

10. Make the distracters plausible and attractive to the uninformed. The distracters in a multiple-choice item should be so appealing to the student who lacks the knowledge called for by the item that he selects one of the distracters in preference to the correct answer. This is the ideal, of course, but one toward which the test maker must work continually. The art of constructing good multiple-choice items depends heavily on the development of effective distracters.

You can do a number of things to increase the plausibility and attractiveness of distracters:

(a) Use the common misconceptions or errors of students as distracters.
(b) State the alternatives in the language of the student.
(c) Use "good-sounding" words ("accurate," "important," and so forth) in the distracters as well as in the correct answer.
(d) Make the distracters similar to the correct answer in both length and complexity of wording.
(e) Use extraneous clues in the distracters, such as stereotyped phrasing, scientific-sounding answers, and verbal associations with the stem of the item. But don't overuse these clues to the point where they become ineffective.
(f) Make the alternatives homogeneous, but in doing so beware of fine discriminations that are educationally insignificant.

The greater plausibility resulting from the use of more homogeneous alternatives can be seen in the improved version of the following item.

Example

Poor: Obtaining a dependable ranking of students is of major concern when using:

*A. norm-referenced summative tests.
B. behavior descriptions.
C. check lists.
D. questionnaires.

Better: Obtaining a dependable ranking of students is of major concern when using:

*A. norm-referenced summative tests.
B. teacher-made diagnostic tests.
C. mastery achievement tests.
D. criterion-referenced formative tests.

The improved version not only increases the plausibility of the distracters; it also calls for a type of discrimination that is more educationally significant.

11. Vary the relative length of the correct answer to eliminate length as a clue. There is a tendency for the correct answer to be longer than the alternatives because of the need to qualify statements to make them unequivocally correct. This, of course, provides a clue to the test-wise student. Learning this fact, the inexperienced test maker frequently makes a special effort to avoid ever having the correct answer longer than the other alternatives. This, of course, also provides a clue, and the alert student soon learns to dismiss the longest alternative as a possible answer.

The relative length of the correct answer can be removed as a clue by varying it in such a manner that no apparent pattern is provided. That is, it should sometimes be longer, sometimes shorter, and sometimes of equal length—but never consistently or predominantly of one relative length. In some cases, it is more desirable to make the alternatives approximately equal length by adjusting the distracters rather than the correct answer:

Example

Poor: One advantage of multiple-choice items over essay questions is that they:

A. measure more complex outcomes.
B. depend more on recall.
C. require less time to score.
*D. provide for a more extensive sampling of course content.

Better: One advantage of multiple-choice items over essay questions is that they:
A. provide for the measurement of more complex learning outcomes.
B. place greater emphasis on the recall of factual information.
C. require less time for test preparation and scoring.
*D. provide for a more extensive sampling of course content.

Lengthening the distracters, as was done in the improved version, both removes length as a clue and increases the plausibility of the distracters, which are now more similar to the correct answer in complexity of wording.

12. Avoid using the alternative "all of the above," and use "none of the above" with extreme caution. When the test maker is having difficulty in locating a sufficient number of distracters, she frequently resorts to the use of "all of the above" or "none of the above" as the final option. These special alternatives are seldom used appropriately and almost always render the item less effective than it would be without them.

The inclusion of "all of the above" as an option makes it possible to answer the item on the basis of partial information. Since the student is to select only one answer, he can detect "all of the above" as the correct choice simply by noting that two of the alternatives are correct. He can also detect it as a wrong answer by recognizing that at least one of the alternatives is incorrect; of course, his chances of guessing the correct answer from the remaining choices then increase proportionately. Another difficulty with this option is that some students, recognizing that the first choice is correct, will select it without reading the remaining alternatives.

Obviously, the use of "none of the above" is not possible with the best-answer type of multiple-choice item, since the alternatives vary in appropriateness and the criterion of absolute correctness is not applicable. When used as the right answer in a correct-answer type of item, this option may be measuring nothing more than the ability to detect incorrect answers. Recognizing that certain answers are wrong is no guarantee that the student knows what is correct. For example, a student may be able to answer the following item correctly without being able to name the categories in the taxonomy:

Example

Poor: Which of the following is a category in the taxonomy of the cognitive domain?
- A. Critical thinking.
- B. Scientific thinking.
- C. Reasoning ability.
- *D. None of above.

All the student needs to know to answer this item correctly is that the taxonomy categories are new and different from those that she has commonly associated with intellectual skills. Items such as this provide rather poor evidence for judging a student's achievement.

The alternative "none of the above" is probably used most widely with computational problems that are presented in multiple-choice form. The publishers of standardized achievement tests have resorted to multiple-choice items for such problems in order to make machine scoring possible, and they have resorted to the alternative "none of the above" in order to reduce the likelihood of the student estimating the answer without performing the entire computation. Although this use of "none of the above" may be defensible, there is seldom a need to use multiple-choice items for computational problems in classroom tests. The supply-type item, which requires the student to solve the problems and record his answers, provides the most direct and useful measure of computational skill. This is another case in which it is desirable to switch from multiple-choice items to another item type in order to obtain more effective measurement.

13. Vary the position of the correct answer in a random manner. The correct answer should appear in each alternative position about the same number of times, but its placement should not follow a pattern that may be apparent to the person taking the test. The student who detects that the correct answer never appears in the same position more than twice in a row, or that A is the correct answer on every fourth item, is likely to obtain a higher score than her knowledge would warrant. Such clues can be avoided by random placement of the correct answer.

The easiest way to randomly assign the position of the correct answer in a multiple-choice item is to develop a code with the aid of a book: simply open any book at random place, look at the right-hand page, and let the last digit of the page number determine the placement of the correct answer. Since the right-hand page always ends in an odd number, the code might be as follows: the digit 1 indicates that the correct answer will be placed in position A, 3 = B, 5 = C, 7 = D, and 9 = E.

Sufficient variation without a discernible pattern might also be obtained by simply placing the responses in alphabetical order, based on the first letter in each, and letting the correct answer fall where it will.

When the alternative responses are numbers, they should always be listed in order of size, preferably in ascending order. This will eliminate the possibility of a clue, such as the correct answer being the only one that is not in numerical order.

14. Control the difficulty of the item either by varying the problem in the stem or by changing the alternatives. It is usually preferable to increase item difficulty by increasing the level of knowledge called for by making the problem more complex. However, it is also possible to increase difficulty by making the alternatives more homogeneous. When this is done, care must be taken that the finer discriminations called for are educationally significant and are in harmony with the learning outcomes to be measured.

15. Make certain each item is independent of the other items in the test. Occasionally, information given in the stem of one item will help the students answer another item. This can be remedied easily by a careful review of the items before they are assembled into a test.

A different type of problem occurs when the correct answer to an item depends upon knowing the correct answer to the item preceding it. The student who is unable to answer the first item, of course, has no basis for responding to the second. Such chains of interlocking items should be avoided. Each item should be an independently scorable unit.

16. Use an efficient item format. The alternatives should be listed on separate lines, under one another, like the examples in this chapter. This makes the alternatives easy to read and compare. It also contributes to ease of scoring since the letters of the alternatives all appear on the left side of the page. A copy of the test can be used as a scoring stencil: simply circle the letters of the correct answers on the copy; then place the copy next to the student's paper so that the columns of letters correspond.

The use of letters in front of the alternatives is preferable to the use of numbers, since numerical answers in numbered items may be confusing to the students.

When writing the item, follow the normal rules of grammar. If the stem of the item is a question, each alternative should begin with a capital letter and end with a period or other terminal punctuation mark. The period should be omitted with numerical answers, however, so that they will not be confused with decimal points. When the stem is an incomplete statement, each alternative should begin with a lower-case letter and end with whatever terminal punctuation mark is appropriate.

The above sixteen rules for constructing multiple-choice items are stated rather dogmatically, as an aid to the beginner. As experience in test construction is obtained, it will soon be noted that there are exceptions to some of the rules and that minor modifications of other rules may be desirable. Until the gaining of such experience, however, the novice will find that following these rules closely will yield test items of fairly high quality.

Constructing True–False Items

The true-false item is simply a declarative statement that the student must judge as true or false. There are modifications of this basic form in which the student must respond "yes" or "no," "agree" or "disagree," "right" or "wrong," "fact" or "opinion," and the like. Such variations are usually given the more general name of *alternative-response* items. In any event, this item type is characterized by the fact that only two responses are possible.

Example

T *F True-false items are classified as a supply-type item.

In some cases the student is asked first to judge each statement as true or false, and then to change the false statements so that they are true. When this is done, a portion of each statement is underlined to indicate the part that can be changed. In the example above, for instance, the words "supply-type" would be underlined. The key parts of true statements, of course, must also be underlined.

Contrary to popular belief, the true-false item is one of the most difficult items to construct. Since it calls for an unqualified judgment that a statement is true or false, the statement must be unquestionably true or clearly false. To construct such items and have them measure important knowledge outcomes requires great skill. In most areas of knowledge, the more important statements must be qualified to make them absolutely true and the qualifiers provide obvious clues. The test maker must resort frequently to the use of more specific and less important factual information in order to obtain properly stated items.

Since only two choices are possible, the uninformed student has a fifty-fifty chance of guessing the answer. This limits the range of scores on the test, and thus reduces its effectiveness as a measuring instrument. The use of two choices poses other problems. When a student marks a true statement false, there is no means of determining what misconception she had in mind. Thus, the true-false item lacks the diagnostic features of the multiple-choice item, where the selection of an incorrect alternative provides clues to the misconception held by the student. Also, when a student correctly marks a false statement false, there is no assurance that she knows the true version of the statement. The item in the above example, for instance, might be marked false by a student who thinks true-false items should be classified as a recall-type item (a not uncommon error). This type of difficulty is avoided with multiple-choice items, since each such item requires the student to select the correct, or best, answer, and *not merely to identify an incorrect answer as incorrect.*

Despite the limitations of the true-false item, there are situations where it should be used. Whenever there are only two possible responses, the true-false item, or some adaptation of it, is likely to provide the most effective measure. Situations of this type include making a simple "yes" or "no" response in classifying objects, determining whether a rule does or does not apply, distinguishing fact from opinion, and indicating whether arguments are relevant or irrelevant. As we indicated earlier, the best procedure is to use the true-false, or alternative-response, item only when the multiple-choice form is inappropriate.

RULES FOR CONSTRUCTING TRUE-FALSE ITEMS

1. Include only one central, significant idea in each statement. The main point of the item should be an important one, and it should be in a prominent position in the statement. The true-false decision should not depend on some subordinate point or trivial detail. The use of several ideas in each statement should generally be avoided because these tend to be confusing and are more apt to measure reading ability than the intended knowledge outcome.

2. Word the statement so precisely that it can unequivocally be judged true or false. True statements should be true under all circumstances, and yet free of qualifiers ("may," "possible," and so on), which might provide clues. This requires the use of precise words and the avoidance of such vague terms as "seldom," "frequently," and "often." The same care, of course, must also be given to false statements so that their falsity is not too readily apparent from differences in wording.

3. Keep the statements short, and use simple language structure. Short, simple statements will increase the likelihood that the point of the item is clear, and that passing or failing it will be determined by the student's knowledge. As we noted earlier, long, involved statements tend to measure reading comprehension, which, of course, defeats the intended purpose of the measurement.

4. Use negative statements sparingly, and avoid double negatives. Negative statements are frequently misread as positive statements because the "no" or "not" is overlooked so easily. Thus, negative statements should be used only when the learning outcome requires it (for example, when emphasizing the avoidance of a harmful practice), and then the negative words should be underlined or written in capital letters.

Double negatives are confusing, and statements using them can usually be restated in positive form. For example, the statement "Correction for guessing is not a practice that should never be used" simply means "Correction for guessing is a practice that should sometimes be used."

5. Statements of opinion should be attributed to some source. Statements of opinion are not true or false by themselves, and it is poor instructional practice to have students respond to them as if they were factual statements. Obviously, the only way students could mark such items correctly would be to agree with the opinion of the test maker. When the opinion is attributed to a particular individual or organization, the item becomes a measure of how well the student knows the beliefs or values of that individual or organization. Opinion statements, of course, may be used without modification if the student is asked to distinguish between statements of fact and statements of opinion.

6. Avoid extraneous clues to the answer. There are a number of *specific determiners* that provide verbal clues to the truth or falsity of an item. Statements that include such absolutes as "always," "never," "all," "none," and "only" tend to be false; statements with qualifiers such as "usually," "may," and "sometimes" tend to be true. Either these verbal clues must be eliminated from the statements, or their use must be balanced between true items and false items.

The length and complexity of the statement might also provide a clue. True statements tend to be longer and more complex than false ones because of their need for qualifiers. Thus, a special effort should be made to equalize true and false statements in these respects.

A tendency to use a disproportionate number of true statements, or false statements, might also be detected and used as a clue. Having approximately, but not exactly, an equal number of each seems to be the best solution. When assembling the test, it is, of course, also necessary to avoid placing the correct answers in some discernible pattern (for instance, T, F, T, F). Random placement will eliminate this possible clue.

Constructing Matching Items

The matching item is simply a modification of the multiple-choice form. Instead of the possible responses being listed underneath each individual stem, a series of stems, called *premises,* is listed in one column and the *responses* are listed in another column:

Example

Directions: Column A contains a list of characteristics of objective test items. On the line at the left of each statement, write the letter of the test item in Column B that best fits the statement. Each response in Column B may be used once, more than once, or not at all.

	Column A	*Column B*
(*D*)	1. Best for measuring computational skills.	A. Matching item.
(C)	2. Least useful for educational diagnosis.	B. Multiple-choice item.
(B)	3. Measures greatest variety of learning outcomes.	C. True-false item.
(D)	4. Most difficult to score objectively.	D. Short-answer item.
(C)	5. Provides the highest score by guessing alone.	
(D)	6. Measures learning at the recall level.	

It can readily be seen that six separate multiple-choice items could be used instead of this matching item, but if this were done, each item would repeat the same four alternatives. Thus, in this example the matching format is a more compact means of measurement. This seems to be the most defensible use of the matching item, and the only condition under which it is desirable to shift from the multiple-choice format to the matching format. Unless *all of the responses* in a matching item *are plausible alternatives for each premise,* the matching format is clearly inappropriate. In any subject-matter area, there are relatively few situations where this condition can be met.

RULES FOR CONSTRUCTING MATCHING ITEMS

1. Include only homogeneous material in each matching item. In our sample item above, we included *only* objective test items and their characteristics. Similarly, an item might include *only* authors and their works, scientists and their discoveries, or historical events and their dates. Such homogeneity is necessary in order that all responses may be plausible.

2. Keep the lists of items short and place the brief responses on the right. A short list of items will save reading time, make it easier for the student to locate the answer, and increase the likelihood that the responses will be homogeneous and plausible. Placing the brief responses on the right also saves reading time.

3. Use a larger, or smaller, number of responses than premises, and permit the responses to be used more than once. Both an uneven match and the possibility of using each response more than once reduces the guessing factor. As we noted earlier, proper use of the matching form requires that *all responses be plausible alternatives for each premise.* This, of course, dictates that each response be eligible for the reuse.

4. Specify in the directions the basis for matching, and indicate that each response may be used once, more than once, or not at all. This will clarify the task for all students and prevent any misunderstanding. Take care, however, not to make the directions too long and involved. The previous example illustrates adequate directions.

Constructing Short–Answer Items

The short-answer (or completion) item is the only objective item type that requires the examinee to supply, rather than select, the answer. Its make-up is similar to a well-stated multiple-choice item without the alternatives. Thus, it consists of a question or incomplete statement to which the examinee responds by providing the appropriate words, numbers, or symbols:

Example

What are the incorrect responses in a multiple-choice item called? (Distracters)

(or)

The incorrect responses in a multiple-choice item are called (distracters).

This item type also includes computational problems and any other simple item form in which the answer is to be supplied rather than selected.

There are two major problems in constructing short-answer items. First, it is extremely difficult to phrase the question or incomplete statement so that only one answer is correct. In our example above, for instance, a student might respond with any one of a number of answers that could be defended as appropriate. He might write "incorrect alternatives," "wrong answers," "inappropriate options," "decoys," "foils," or some other equally descriptive response. Second, there is the problem of spelling. If credit is given only when the answer is spelled correctly, the poor spellers will be prevented from showing their true level of achievement and the test scores will become an uninterpretable mixture of knowledge and spelling skill. On the other hand, if attempts are made to ignore spelling during the scoring process, there is still the problem of deciding whether a badly spelled word represents the intended answer. This, of course, introduces an element of subjectivity, which tends to make the scores less dependable as measures of achievement.

Due to the above weaknesses, the short-answer item should be reserved for those special situations where supplying the answer is a necessary part of the learning outcome to be measured—for example, where the intent is to have students *recall* the information, where computational problems are used, or where a selection-type item would make the answer obvious. In these situations, the use of the short-answer item can be defended despite its shortcomings.

RULES FOR CONSTRUCTING SHORT-ANSWER ITEMS

1. State the item so that only a single, brief answer is possible. This requires great skill in phrasing and the use of precise terms. What appears to be a simple, clear question to the test maker can frequently be answered in many different ways, as we noted with the previous sample item.

2. Start with a direct question, and switch to an incomplete statement only when greater conciseness is possible by doing so. The use of a direct question increases the likelihood that the problem will be stated clearly and that only one answer will be appropriate. Also, incomplete statements tend to be less ambiguous when they are based on problems that were first stated in question form.

3. The words to be supplied should relate to the main point of the statement. Avoid asking students to respond to unimportant or minor aspects of a statement, and leave blanks only for key words. Students should not be expected to supply such words as "the" and "an."

4. Place the blanks at the end of the statement. This permits the student to read the complete problem before coming to the blank. Starting with a direct question, as suggested above, will make it easier to construct the incomplete statements.

5. Avoid extraneous clues to the answer. The use of the indefinite articles "a" or "an" at the end of an incomplete statement is apt to provide a clue to the answer. The length of the answer blank might also provide a clue, unless the length is uniform from one item to another.

6. For numerical answers, indicate the degree of precision expected and the units in which they are to be expressed. This will clarify the task for the student and make scoring easier. If the learning outcome requires students to know the type of unit in common use and the degree of precision expected, this rule must, of course, be disregarded.

Additional Reading

BLOOM, B. S., ed., et al., *Taxonomy of Educational Objectives: Cognitive Domain.* New York: David McKay Co., Inc., 1956. Contains illustrative objective test items for each type of knowledge outcome.

BLOOM, B. S., J. T. HASTINGS, and G. F. MADAUS, *Handbook on Formative and Summative Evaluation of Student Learning.* New York: McGraw-Hill Book Company, 1971. Chapters 13 to 23 contain illustrative test items for various subject areas. All are keyed to the categories in the Taxonomy (Bloom et al., 1956).

GRONLUND, N. E., *Measurement and Evaluation in Teaching* (3rd ed.), Chaps. 7 and 8. New York: Macmillan Publishing Co., Inc., 1976. Rules for constructing the various types of objective test items are illustrated by numerous sample test items.

WESMAN, A. G., "Writing the Test Item," in *Educational Measurement* (2nd ed.), ed. R. L. Thorndike, Chap. 4. Washington, D.C.: American Council on Education, 1971. A comprehensive treatment of item writing.

4

Constructing Objective Tests of Complex Achievement

Complex learning outcomes ranging from the lowest level of understanding. . . . to the higher levels of intellectual skill. . . . can be measured by objective test items. Both simple and complex item types are useful. . . . and various adaptations can be designed to fit particular learning outcomes.

In the last chapter, we limited our discussion to the construction of objective test items that measure knowledge outcomes—that is, to the design of items that appraise the student's ability to remember material in essentially the same form in which it was learned. Such items require the student to either remember the information and select the appropriate response from those given, or to recall and supply the answer. They do not require him to understand, interpret, or use the information in any way. Many teachers limit the use of objective test items to such relatively simple knowledge outcomes, but this is a needless restriction. With proper care, objective test items can be designed to measure a wide range of complex learning outcomes.

Test items that measure complex achievement are characterized by a certain amount of novelty. For example, whereas a knowledge item might require a student to identify a textbook definition of a term, a complex measure may require him to identify a modified version of it or an illustration of its proper use. Similarly, whereas a knowledge item might call for the identification of a previously learned statement of a principle, a complex measure may demand an interpretation or application of the principle. Thus, items that measure complex achievement seek evidence that the student has attached meanings to his knowledge and that he can use this knowledge effectively in dealing with situations that are new to him.

Many complex learning outcomes can be measured with single, self-contained test items like those described in the last chapter; in this case, the task of the test maker is mainly to introduce an element of novelty into the problem situations and to adapt the items to the intended outcomes. Other learning outcomes, however, are best measured by more elaborate and complex item types. The use of these two formats, the single-item and the complex-item, will be discussed in turn.

Taxonomy Categories and the Use of the Single–Item Format

The multiple-choice item and modifications of the alternative-response item are the most generally useful formats for measuring complex achievement. The rules of construction are the same as those described in the last chapter, of course, but greater skill is required in identifying and defining the problem situations. Also, the increased complexity of the tasks presented and the inclusion of some novelty create a greater need for careful phrasing of the items.

To demonstrate the wide variety of complex learning outcomes that can be measured with the single-item format, we'll present illustrative test items for the major categories of intellectual skills and abilities listed in the cognitive domain of the Taxonomy of Educational Objectives (Bloom et al., 1956). Recall that these categories are comprehension, application, analysis, synthesis, and evaluation.[1] No attempt will be made to illustrate all of the possible item types. Further illustrations may be obtained from the references listed at the end of the chapter.

COMPREHENSION ITEMS

Comprehension items measure at the lowest level of understanding. They determine whether the student has grasped the meaning of the material, without requiring her to apply it, analyze it, or relate it to other material. Comprehension can be measured by requiring students to *translate* material from one form to another, to *interpret* the meaning of material, or to *extrapolate*—that is, extend the meaning beyond the data presented. These three types of comprehension are hierarchical in nature,

[1] The following brief descriptions of these categories are simply a summary of the more extensive descriptions given in the Taxonomy of Educational Objectives (Bloom et al., 1956). For further information, consult the original source.

translation being the simplest and extrapolation the most complex. Thus, interpretation includes translation, and extrapolation includes both of these.

The following test items illustrate the measurement of learning outcomes representing each of these types of comprehension.

Example

Outcome: Ability to identify the meaning of a term (Translation).

1. Which one of the following is closest in meaning to the term *taxonomy?*
   *A. Classification.
   B. Construction.
   C. Evaluation.
   D. Translation.
2. Which one of the following true-false statements contains a *specific determiner?*
   A. America is a continent.
   B. America was discovered in 1492.
   *C. America has some big industries.
   D. America's population is increasing.

Example

Outcome: Ability to grasp the meaning of an idea (Interpretation).

1. The statement, "Test reliability is a necessary but not a sufficient condition of test validity," means that
   A. a reliable test will have a certain degree of validity.
   *B. a valid test will have a certain degree of reliability.
   C. a reliable test may be completely invalid and a valid test completely unreliable.

Example

Outcome: Ability to identify the explanation of a phenomenon (Interpretation).

1. If a true-false test is to replace a multiple-choice test, the number of items will have to be greater. Why?
   *A. To maintain the same reliability.
   B. To maintain the same level of difficulty.
   C. To maintain the same coverage of subject matter.
   D. To allow for a larger number of true statements than false statements.

Example

Outcome: Ability to predict the most probable effect of an action (Extrapolation).

1. What is most likely to happen to the reliability of the scores on a multiple-choice test in which the number of alternatives for each item is changed from four to five?
   *A. It will increase.
   B. It will decrease.
   C. It will stay the same.

Of course, these examples would represent measurement at the comprehension level only if the situations were new to the students. If the solutions to these particular problems were encountered during instruction, the items would have to be classified under knowledge outcomes.

Learning outcomes in the area of translation can be measured readily by single-item tests. However, outcomes in the areas of interpretation and extrapolation are measured more easily by complex-item types, in which it is possible to base a series of items on a given paragraph, table, map, graph, or picture. A discussion of such items will be presented later in this chapter.

APPLICATION ITEMS

Application items also measure understanding, but at a higher level in the cognitive domain than that of comprehension. Here, the student must demonstrate that he not only grasps the meaning of information but can also apply it to concrete situations that are new to him. Thus, application items determine the extent to which students can transfer their learning and use it effectively in solving new problems. Such items may call for the application of various aspects of knowledge, such as facts, principles, rules, methods, and theories. Both comprehension and application items are adaptable to practically all areas of subject matter, and they are the basic means of measuring understanding.

The following examples illustrate the use of objective test items for measuring learning outcomes at the application level.

Example

Outcome: Ability to recognize examples of properly stated learning outcomes (Application of facts and principles).

Directions: Indicate which of the following learning outcomes are properly stated in behavioral terms; circle Y for yes and N for no.

Y N* 1. Student learns the purposes of achievement testing.
Y N* 2. Student develops an appreciation of objective testing.
*Y N 3. Student explains the advantages of using a table of specifications.
*Y N 4. Student identifies errors in test items.

Example

Outcome: Ability to improve test items (Application of rules of procedure).

Directions: Read the following test item and then indicate the best change to make to improve the item.

1. Which one of the following types of learning outcomes is most difficult to evaluate objectively?
   1. A concept.
   2. An application.
   3. An appreciation.
   4. None of the above.

The best change to make in the above item would be to:

A. change the stem to incomplete-statement form.
B. use letters instead of numbers for each alternative.
C. remove the indefinite article "a" and "an" from the alternatives.
*D. replace "None of the above" with "An interpretation."

As with most other types of complex achievement, learning outcomes at the application level can frequently be measured more efficiently by a series of test items based on a common situation. Essay questions, of course, can also be used, and for complex situations they may be the most desirable item type. The single-item format, however, can be used effectively to measure a variety of specific types of application and should be used where appropriate.

When constructing application items, take care to select problems that the student has not encountered previously and cannot solve on the basis of general knowledge alone. The item should be designed so that it calls for application of the particular facts, principles, or procedures indicated in the learning outcome.

ANALYSIS ITEMS

Analysis, the breaking down of material into its component parts, includes (1) identification of the parts (*analysis of elements*), (2) identification of the relationships between parts (*analysis of relationships*), and

(3) identification of the way the elements are organized (*analysis of organizational principles*). These three types of analysis are listed in order of increasing complexity.

The *analysis of elements,* the lowest level of analysis, includes such abilities as recognizing unstated assumptions, distinguishing between fact and opinion, and distinguishing conclusions from the facts that support them. Specific skills such as these can be measured with the single-item format.

Example

Outcome: Ability to recognize unstated assumptions.

1. The author of a recent book on measurement claims that students will obtain correct answers on 50 percent of the items in a true-false test by guessing. Which one of the following assumptions is the author making?
   A. Students will make some informed guesses.
   *B. Students will guess blindly.
   C. Students' guessing will be aided by some specific determiners.
   D. Students' guessing will be aided by both partial information and some specific determiners.

The *analysis of relationships* includes such outcomes as identifying relationships between ideas, recognizing cause-effect relations, and distinguishing between relevant and irrelevant arguments.

Example

Outcome: Identifying relations between ideas.

1. Read the following two statements and select the answer that best explains their relationship.
   One: Other things being equal, a longer test is more reliable than a shorter test.
   Two: Other things being equal, a fifty-item multiple-choice test is more reliable than a fifty-item true-false test.
   The relationship between these statements can best be expressed as follows:
   A. The situation in statement two contradicts the principle in statement one.
   *B. The situation in statement two can be explained by the principle in statement one.
   C. The situation in statement two neither contradicts nor can be explained by the principle in statement one.

In this example, the student must recognize that increasing the number of alternatives in the items of a test produces the same effect as lengthening the test.

The *analysis of organizational principles* requires the student to recognize or infer the form, pattern, or structure that is implicit in a communication (that is, a work of literature, a musical composition, or a painting). Thus, it includes the ability to identify such things as a writer's purpose, point of view, bias, persuasive techniques, and literary form. This is the most complex level of analysis, and one that is perhaps necessary for a full understanding of works of literature, music, and art; it tends to have less significance in other areas.

The following example is based on the material presented in this book (up to this point).

Example

Outcome: Ability to recognize a writer's point of view.

1. Which one of the following statements best expresses the point of view of the author (of this book) toward achievement testing?
   A. Objectivity should be maintained even if some of the learning outcomes are measured less directly.
   *B. Learning outcomes should be measured directly even if less objective measures must be used.
   C. Neither measuring the learning outcomes directly nor maintaining objectivity is as important as following closely the rules for constructing test items.

The examples presented in this section measure only the most elementary forms of behavior called for in analysis. More advanced examples would present the student with a complete and more complex set of materials to be analyzed: a literary selection, a poem, a description of an experiment, a painting, or some other material that is new to her. Appropriate questions would then require the student to analyze all aspects (elements, relationships, and structure) of the given material. Single items such as the three previous examples are useful mainly for determining whether students have the needed skills and understandings to effectively approach a more comprehensive task of analysis. Of course, they also measure learning outcomes that are significant in their own right.

The material in items that measure analysis outcomes must be new to the students, and the test questions should require more than the simple application of analysis skills. Properly constructed analysis items require students to demonstrate a deeper understanding of the material than that called forth by comprehension and application items.

APPRAISING SYNTHESIS OUTCOMES

Synthesis involves putting parts together to form a *product* that is new to the student. Thus, the process assumes a certain amount of creative activity, the amount of which is determined by the specific task. Three types of synthesis have been proposed. These are distinguished primarily on the basis of the *product* resulting from the synthesis: (1) the student may be asked to produce *a unique communication,* such as an essay, a short story, a poem, a musical composition, or a speech; (2) the student may be asked to produce *a plan or proposed set of operations,* such as a plan for an experiment, specifications for making an article of clothing or furniture, or a proposal for some scientific process or social action; (3) the student may be asked to produce *a set of abstract relations,* such as hypotheses that account for diverse phenomena, a simple theory, or a conceptual scheme for classifying things or events.

Since the process of synthesis emphasizes the student's ability to create and organize ideas, objective test items play only a minor role in this area. Such items can be used to measure individual aspects of writing skill, such as the ability to select the wording that best expresses an idea, or the ability to arrange scrambled sentences into a coherent paragraph, but these constitute only minor aspects of the larger act of synthesis. Objective test items can probably be defended best on the grounds that students' responses to such items have been shown to relate substantially to their writing ability as measured with essays (Godshalk, Swineford, and Coffman, 1966). For most classroom purposes, however, it is probably more desirable to have the students write the essay than to measure their writing ability indirectly by using objective items.

Appraising learning outcomes at the synthesis level of the cognitive domain depends primarily on product evaluation. Typically, the student is asked to produce something that requires the type of synthesis reflected in the instructional objectives, and the quality of the resulting product is judged in terms of clearly defined criteria. In the area of achievement testing, for example, the student might be requested to state instructional objectives for a unit of work or construct specific types of test items (production of a unique communication), prepare a set of specifications for an achievement test (production of a proposed set of operations), or develop a system for classifying learning outcomes that is unique to a particular area of study (production of a set of abstract relations). The resulting product would be appraised in light of clearly established criteria (such as the rules and standards for test construction), the novelty of the content and structure of the product, and the usefulness of the product for the intended purpose.

Tasks designed to measure synthesis outcomes should neither require strict adherence to a set of step-by-step procedures nor permit completely free creative expression. A happy medium, one that provides for some creativity but also includes limits set by commonly accepted conventions and minimum standards, seems most appropriate. The particular field of study and the instructional objectives will, of course, largely determine this balance.

APPRAISING EVALUATION OUTCOMES

Evaluation involves consciously judging, with the aid of definite criteria, the value of a thing for a given purpose. Both the consciousness of the judgment and the use of criteria are essential features, since they distinguish the cognitive type of *evaluation* stressed in the taxonomy from those emotionally based decisions that fall in the *opinion* category. Thus, evaluation as defined here is the most complex of the cognitive behaviors. It includes some elements of knowledge, comprehension, analysis, and synthesis, plus the use of criteria and value judgments.

Evaluation outcomes may be divided into two types: (1) those in which the judgment is based on *internal evidence,* such as accuracy, consistency, and logical order, and (2) those in which the judgment is based on *external criteria,* such as the commonly accepted standards for a given type of product, or the efficiency, economy, and utility with which the product serves a particular purpose. In both types of evaluative judgments, either the criteria may be given to the student or the student may be required to supply them.

Some of the specific aspects of the evaluation process can be measured with objective test items. For example, outcomes such as the ability to detect logical fallacies in arguments, the ability to recognize appropriate criteria to use in a given situation, the ability to detect various types of errors, and the ability to identify means-ends relationships can be measured objectively. The measurement of such individual aspects of evaluation, however, does not include the analysis and synthesis skills required in an overall evaluation of a work. Thus, such aspects are probably classified more appropriately at the application level.

A comprehensive appraisal of learning outcomes at the evaluation level of the cognitive domain would demand that the student be given a complete work and be required to (1) analyze it, (2) make specific judgments concerning each of its various parts, in accordance with the specific criteria used, and (3) synthesize the results into an overall judgment of the work's value for a given purpose. In the area of achievement testing, for example, the student might be given a complete achievement test that he is expected to evaluate in terms of internal evidence (conciseness of directions, clarity and arrangement of items, legibility, and so on) and in terms of external criteria (relevance to learning outcomes, representativeness of sampling, and so forth). As we indicated earlier, the student may be given the list of criteria to use, or he may be asked to provide his own. He would be expected to include in his final report a detailed analysis of the errors and shortcomings he encountered, the specific judgments he made, a summary of the overall evaluation, and specific reasons for each of his evaluative judgments.

Cognitive abilities at the evaluation level, as with those at the synthesis level, are likely to be appraised most effectively when the student is asked to evaluate a complete work. How successfully he has achieved the outcomes at the evaluation level can then be determined by judging the quality of his written report.

Use of Complex-Item Types

Complex learning outcomes can frequently be measured more effectively by basing a series of test items upon the same piece of introductory material. This may be a paragraph, a table, a chart, a graph, a map, or a picture. The test items that follow the introductory material may be designed to call forth any of the intellectual abilities and skills described in the Taxonomy that can be measured objectively. Multiple-choice items and alternative-response items are widely used with this type exercise.

The following example illustrates the use of multiple-choice items. Note that this item type makes it possible to measure a variety of learning outcomes based on the same introductory material. In this example, item 1 measures the *ability to recognize unstated assumptions,* item 2 the *ability to interpret,* and item 3 the *ability to identify relationships.*

Example

Directions: Read the following comments that a teacher made about testing. Then answer the questions that follow the comments by circling the letter of the best answer.

"Students go to school to learn, not to take tests. In addition, tests cannot be used to indicate a student's absolute level of learning. All tests can do is rank students in order of achievement, and this relative ranking is influenced by guessing, bluffing, and the subjective opinions of the teacher doing the scoring. The teaching-learning process would benefit if we did away with tests and depended on student self-evaluation."

1. Which one of the following unstated assumptions is this teacher making?
   A. Students go to school to learn.
   B. Teachers use essay tests primarily.
   *C. Tests make no contribution to learning.
   D. Tests do not indicate a student's absolute level of learning.
2. Which one of the following types of tests is this teacher talking about primarily?
   A. Diagnostic test.
   B. Formative test.
   C. Pretest.
   *D. Summative test.
3. Which one of the following propositions is most essential to the teacher's conclusion?
   *A. Effective self-evaluation does not require the use of tests.
   B. Tests place students in rank order only.
   C. Test scores are influenced by factors other than achievement.
   D. Students do not go to school to take tests.

The next example uses a modified version of the alternative-response form. This is frequently called a *key-type* item because a common set of alternatives is used in responding to each question. Note that the key-type item is devoted entirely to the measurement of one learning outcome. In this example, the item measures the *ability to recognize warranted and unwarranted inferences.*

Example

Directions: Paragraph A contains a description of the testing practices of Mr. Smith, a high school teacher. Read this description and each of the statements that follow it. Mark each statement to indicate the type of INFERENCE that can be drawn about it from the material in the paragraph. Place the appropriate letter in front of each statement, using the following KEY:

T: the statement may be INFERRED as TRUE.
F: the statement may be INFERRED as UNTRUE.
N: NO INFERENCE may be drawn about the statement from the material in the paragraph.

Paragraph A

Approximately one week before a test is to be given, Mr. Smith goes through the textbook carefully and constructs multiple-choice items based on the material in the book. He always uses the exact wording of the textbook for the correct answer so that there will be no question concerning the answer's correctness. He is careful to include some test items from each chapter. After the test is given, he lists the scores on the blackboard, from high to low, and tells each student his or her score. He does not return the test papers to the students, but he offers to answer any questions they might have about the test. He puts the items from each test into a test file, which he is building for future use.

Statements on Paragraph A

(T) 1. Mr. Smith's tests measure a limited range of learning outcomes.
(F) 2. Some of Mr. Smith's test items measure at the understanding level.
(N) 3. Mr. Smith's tests measure a balanced sample of subject matter.
(N) 4. Mr. Smith uses the type of test item that is best for his purpose.
(T) 5. Students can determine where they rank in the distribution of scores on Mr. Smith's tests.
(F) 6. Mr. Smith's testing practices are likely to motivate students to overcome their weaknesses.

Key-type items are fairly easy to develop and can be related directly to specific learning outcomes. The key categories can, of course, be reused simply by changing the introductory material and the statements. Thus, key-type items provide a standard framework for test preparation. Other common key categories include the following: (1) the argument is relevant, irrelevant, or neither; (2) the statement is supported by the evidence, refuted by the evidence, or neither; (3) the assumption is necessary, or unnecessary; (4) the conclusion is valid, it is invalid, or its validity cannot be determined. Although such standard key categories should not be applied perfunctorily, they can provide guidelines that simplify the construction of this more complex item type.

CONSTRUCTING COMPLEX-ITEM TYPES

The effectiveness of complex items such as those illustrated above depends on the care with which the introductory material is selected and the skill with which the series of dependent items is prepared. In selecting introductory material, keep in mind the learning outcomes to be measured. The material should be complex enough to make possible the testing of the intended skills and abilities, but not so complex that it introduces a level of reasoning or reading comprehension that interferes with the intended measurement. A sound procedure is to select written material from magazines or books at the students' level and rewrite it to fit the learning outcomes to be measured and the reading ability of the slower students. Where possible, it is also desirable to use tables, charts, graphs, maps, pictures, or cartoons. Some learning outcomes, such as the ability to recognize valid conclusions, may be measured as effectively with one type of material as with another. In such cases, the type of material that places the least emphasis on reading ability should be favored.

To measure complex achievement effectively, the introductory material must, of course, be new to the students. It should not be material that was discussed in class, or that is included in the textbook or the assigned readings. On the other hand, the form of the material must be familiar to the students. For instance, if they are to be asked to identify relations between points on a graph, it will be necessary to use a type of graph with which they have had some experience.

The test items that are based on the introductory material should call forth the type of behavior specified in the learning outcome (interpretation, extrapolation, analysis of relationships, and so forth). This requires careful phrasing of the questions and special attention to two cautions. First, *the answer to an item should not be given directly in the material,* since some mental process beyond "recognition of a stated fact" is required in measures of intellectual skills. Second, *it should not be possible to answer the question without the introductory material.* If an item can be answered by students on the basis of general knowledge, it is not measuring their ability to interpret or analyze the material. A good check on this type of error is to cover the introductory material and attempt to answer the questions without it.

All of the rules for constructing objective test items that were discussed in the last chapter are applicable to the construction of complex items. Even greater care must be taken to avoid extraneous clues in the latter, however, since complex items seem especially prone to such clues and the clues tend to be more difficult to detect in these items. If the introductory material includes illustrations, special attention should be directed to such things as the size, shape, and position of objects as possible extraneous clues. These clues are frequently overlooked by the test maker, who is concentrating on the intricacies of the mental response required, but not by the unprepared student, who is frantically searching for any solution to the problem.

The greatest help in constructing complex-item types is to review a wide range of sample exercises and the different types of introductory material and different forms of dependent test items included therein. For this purpose, see Bloom et al. (1956), Bloom, Hastings, and Madaus (1971), Gronlund (1976), Educational Testing Service (1973), and Morse and McCune (1971) in the following list of references.

Additional Reading

BLOOM, B. S., ed., et al., *Taxonomy of Educational Objectives: Cognitive Domain.* New York: David McKay Co., Inc., 1956. Contains numerous illustrative items for each category of the Taxonomy.

BLOOM, B. S., J. T. HASTINGS, and G. F. MADAUS, *Handbook on Formative and Summative Evaluation of Student Learning.* New York: McGraw-Hill Book Company, 1971. See Chapters 13 to 23 for illustrative test items in various subject areas. All are keyed to the categories in the Taxonomy.

Educational Testing Service, Test Development Division, *Multiple-Choice Questions: A Close Look.* Princeton, N.J., 1973. Illustrates the use of maps, graphs, diagrams, pictures, and written materials in measuring complex achievement.

GODSHALK, F. I., F. SWINEFORD, and W. E. COFFMAN, *The Measurement of Writing Ability.* New York: College Entrance Examination Board, 1966. Describes studies of the use of both objective and essay items in measuring writing ability.

GRONLUND, N. E., *Measurement and Evaluation in Teaching* (3rd ed.), Chap. 9. New York: Macmillan Publishing Co., Inc., 1976. Presents a variety of complex items and describes the preparation of interpretive exercises.

MORSE, H. T., and G. M. MCCUNE, *Selected Items for the Testing of Study Skills and Critical Thinking.* Washington, D.C.: National Council for the Social Studies, 1971. Presents a wide variety of complex items for measuring thinking skills.

SYND, R. B., and A. J. PICARD, *Behavioral Objectives and Evaluation Measures: Science and Mathematics,* Chap. 10. Columbus, Ohio: Charles E. Merrill Publishers, 1972. Presents numerous illustrative test items for the elementary and secondary school levels.

WESMAN, A. G., "Writing the Test Item," in *Educational Measurement* (2nd ed.), ed. R. L. Thorndike, Chap. 4. Washington, D.C.: American Council on Education, 1971. See pp. 120–28 for a discussion of the construction of interpretive exercises.

5

Constructing Essay Tests

Essay tests are inefficient for measuring knowledge outcomes. . . . but they provide a freedom of response that is needed in measuring certain complex outcomes. . . . These outcomes include the ability to create. . . . to organize. . . . to integrate. . . . to express. . . . and similar behaviors that call for the production and synthesis of ideas.

Objective test items play a prominent role in achievement testing. As we have seen in the last two chapters, they can be used to measure both knowledge outcomes and a variety of intellectual skills and abilities. It is only when we reach the higher-level synthesis and evaluation categories of the Taxonomy of Educational Objectives (Bloom et al., 1956) that objective test items become ineffective or inappropriate. At these levels, and in those areas at the lower levels where producing and organizing the answer is crucial, we must turn to the essay test.

The Nature of the Essay Test

The most notable characteristic of the essay test is the freedom of response it provides. The student is asked a question that requires him to produce his own answer. He is relatively free to decide how to approach the problem, what factual information to use, how to organize his reply, and what degree of emphasis to give to each aspect of his answer. Thus, the essay question places a premium on the ability to produce, integrate, and express ideas. These are the very types of behavior for which the objective test item is so inadequate.

Were it not for some rather serious shortcomings of the essay test, objective items might never have come into existence. One of the essay's major weaknesses is the limited sampling of achievement it provides. Since only a small number of questions can be included in an essay test, the sampling of student achievement is confined to a relatively few areas. Although this may provide for greater depth of measurement in these areas, it is patently impossible to obtain a representative sample of achievement. As a result, the student who has concentrated her study in the areas in which the questions happen to fall will obtain a spuriously high score, whereas the student who has devoted more attention to other areas will receive a lower score than her achievement warrants.

A second shortcoming is concerned with the student's response. Since the student must write the answers to essay questions in his own words, writing ability tends to influence the score he receives. Poor expression and errors in punctuation, spelling, and grammar typically lower the scores assigned to essay answers. This, of course, distorts the scores as a measure of the intended learning outcomes. On the other hand, cleverness in written expression and bluffing tend to inflate the scores assigned to essay answers. Even the student who says nothing but expresses it well is apt to receive some credit. An exaggerated example of this was reported in the literature some years ago. A college test bureau selected a student with special writing skills and sent him into a mid-semester examination in place of a regular student in order to determine how well he could do on an essay test without preparation. The main question called for a critical evaluation of a novel that the student had not read. His answer started out somewhat as follows: "This is not the best novel I have ever read, but neither is it the worst. It has some real strengths, such as the detailed attention given to the development of the main characters. On the other hand, some of the minor characters have not been developed as fully as they might be. . . ." His evaluation continued along this vein. The paper was returned at the next class meeting, along with this comment by the professor: "This is the best evaluation of this novel I have ever read." Although extreme, such experiences illustrate the great difficulty in obtaining an uncontaminated measure of achievement with the essay test.

A third shortcoming, related to the one above, has to do with the subjective nature of the scoring. Variations in the content of the answers from paper to paper tend to cause a shifting of standards during the grading process. Thus, the scoring is not only difficult and time-consuming but also tends to be inconsistent. A number of studies have shown that different raters assign different grades when evaluating the same paper independently, and that a similar variation is obtained when a rater regrades a paper after a period of time (Coffman, 1971). Such unreliability tends to shake our confidence in the use of essay questions as measures of achievement. It should be pointed out, however, that some of the inconsistency in scoring reported in these studies was undoubtedly due to a lack of clarity concerning the type of answer desired and to the absence of definite scoring rules. Studies have shown that essay answers can be graded with a higher degree of reliability when such factors are given careful consideration (Coffman, 1971).

The limitations of the essay test are of such magnitude that it should probably never be used as the sole measure of achievement. On the other hand, essay questions are of such importance in measuring certain learning outcomes that they should probably be used to some degree in most achievement tests. A balanced testing program would include the use of both objective and essay questions, the latter being restricted to those learning outcomes that cannot be measured objectively. Thus, for the measurement of most knowledge outcomes we would use objective test items, because of their greater reliability and the more extensive sampling they afford. For the measurement of such complex learning outcomes as the ability to create, organize, and evaluate ideas, however, we would use essay questions, despite their limitations.

A summary comparison of the merits of objective and essay tests is presented in Table 5.1. As can be seen in this table, both item types are efficient for some purposes and inefficient for others. It is also apparent that the two types tend to complement each other in terms of the types of learning outcomes measured and the effects they are most likely to have on student learning.

Types of Essay Questions

The freedom of response permitted by essay questions varies considerably. A student may be required to give a brief and precise response, or she may be given great freedom in determining the form and scope of her answer. Questions of the first type are commonly called restricted-response questions and those of the second type are called extended-response questions. This is an arbitrary but convenient pair of categories for classifying essay questions.

Table 5.1. *Summary Comparison of Objective and Essay Tests*

	OBJECTIVE TEST	ESSAY TEST
Taxonomy Outcomes Measured	Good for measuring outcomes at the knowledge, comprehension, application, and analysis levels of the Taxonomy; inadequate for synthesis and evaluation outcomes.	Inefficient for knowledge outcomes; good for comprehension, application, and analysis outcomes; best for synthesis and evaluation outcomes.
Sampling of Content	The use of a large number of items results in broad coverage, which makes representative sampling of content feasible.	The use of a relatively small number of items results in limited coverage, which makes representative sampling of content infeasible.
Preparation of Items	Preparation of good items is difficult and time-consuming.	Preparation of good items is difficult, but easier than the preparation of objective items.
Scoring	Objective, simple, and highly reliable.	Subjective, difficult, and less reliable.
Factors that Distort Students' Scores	Reading ability and guessing.	Writing ability and bluffing.
Probable Effect on Learning	Encourages students to remember, interpret, and analyze the ideas of others.	Encourages students to organize, integrate, and express their own ideas.

RESTRICTED-RESPONSE QUESTIONS

The restricted-response question places strict limits on the answer to be given. The boundaries of the subject matter to be considered are usually narrowly defined by the problem, and the specific form of the answer is also commonly indicated (by words such as "list," "define," and "give reasons"). In some cases, the response is limited further by the use of introductory material or by the use of special directions:

Example

Describe the relative merits of objective test items and essay questions for measuring learning outcomes at the comprehension level. Confine your answer to one page.

Example

Mr. Rogers, a ninth-grade science teacher, wants to measure his students' "ability to interpret scientific data" with a papar-and-pencil test.

1. Describe the steps that Mr. Rogers should follow.
2. Give reasons to justify each step.

Restricting the form and scope of the answers to essay questions has both advantages and disadvantages. Such questions can be prepared more easily, related more directly to specific learning outcomes, and scored more easily. On the other hand, however, they provide little opportunity for the student to demonstrate her ability to organize, to integrate, and to develop essentially new patterns of response. The imposed limitations make restricted-response items especially useful for measuring learning outcomes at the comprehension, application, and analysis levels of the Taxonomy. They are of relatively little value for measuring outcomes at the synthesis and evaluation levels. At these levels, the extended-response question provides the more appropriate measure.

EXTENDED-RESPONSE QUESTIONS

The extended-response question gives the student almost unlimited freedom to determine the form and scope of his response. Although in some instances rather rigid practical limits may be imposed, such as time limits or page limits, restrictions on the material to be included in the answer and on the form of the response are held to a minimum. The student must be given sufficient freedom to demonstrate skills of synthesis and evaluation, and just enough control to assure that the intended intellectual skills and abilities will be called forth by the question. Thus, the amount of structure will vary from item to item, depending on the learning outcomes being measured, but the stress will always be on providing as much freedom as the situation permits.

Example

Synthesis Level: For a course that you are teaching, or expect to teach, prepare a complete plan for evaluating student achievement. Be sure to include the procedures you would follow, the instruments you would use, and the reasons for your choices.

Example

Evaluation Level: (The student is given a complete achievement test that includes errors or flaws in the directions, in the test items, and in the arrangement of the items.) Write a critical evaluation of this test, using as evaluative criteria the rules and standards for test construction described in your textbook. Include a detailed analysis of the test's strengths and weaknesses and an evaluation of its overall quality and probable effectiveness.

The extended-response question provides for the creative integration of ideas, the overall evaluation of materials, and a broad approach to problem solving. These are all important learning outcomes, and ones that cannot be measured by other types of test items. The biggest problem, of course, is to evaluate the answers with sufficient reliability to provide a useful measure of learning. This is a difficult and time-consuming task, but the importance of the outcomes would seem to justify the additional care and effort required.

Rules for Constructing Essay Questions

The construction of clear, unambiguous essay questions that call forth the desired responses is a much more difficult task than is commonly presumed. The following rules will not make the task any easier, but their application will result in essay items of higher quality.

1. Use essay questions to measure complex learning outcomes only. Most knowledge outcomes profit little from being measured by essay questions. These outcomes can usually be measured more effectively by objective items, which lack the sampling and scoring problems that essay questions introduce. There may be a few exceptions, as when supplying the answer is a basic part of the learning outcome, but for most knowledge outcomes essay questions simply provide a less reliable measure with no compensating benefits.

At the comprehension, application, and analysis levels of the Taxonomy, both objective tests and essay tests are useful. Even here, though, the objective test would seem to have priority, the essay test being reserved for those situations that require the student to *give* reasons, *explain* relationships, *describe* data, *formulate* conclusions, or in some other way *produce* the appropriate answer. Where supplying the answer is vital, a properly constructed restricted-response question is likely to be most appropriate.

At the synthesis and evaluation levels of the Taxonomy, both the objective test and the restricted-response test have only limited value. These tests may be used to measure some specific aspects of the total process, but the production of a complete work (such as a plan of operation) or an overall evaluation of a work (for instance, an evaluation of a novel or an experiment) requires the use of extended-response questions. It is at this level that the essay form contributes most uniquely.

2. Relate the questions as directly as possible to the learning outcomes being measured. Essay questions will not measure complex learning outcomes unless they are carefully constructed to do so. Each question should be specifically designed to measure one or more well-defined outcomes. Thus, the place to start, as is the case with objective items, is with a precise description of the behavior to be measured. This will help determine both the content and form of the item and will aid in the phrasing of it.

The restricted-response item is related quite easily to a specific learning outcome because it is so highly structured. The limited response expected from the student also makes it possible for the test maker to phrase the question so that its intent is communicated clearly to the student. The extended-response item, however, requires greater freedom of response and typically involves a number of learning outcomes. This makes it more difficult to relate the question to the intended outcomes and to indicate the nature of the desired answer through the phrasing of the question. If the task is prescribed too rigidly in the question, the students' freedom to select, organize, and present the answer is apt to be infringed upon. One practical solution is to indicate to the students the criteria to be used in evaluating the answer. For example, a parenthetical statement such as the following might be added: "Your answer will be evaluated in terms of its comprehensiveness, the relevance of its arguments, the appropriateness of its examples, and the skill with which it is organized." This clarifies the task to the students without limiting their freedom, and makes the item easier to relate to clearly defined learning outcomes.

3. Formulate questions that present a clear task to the student.

Phrasing an essay question so that the desired response is obtained is no simple matter. Selecting precise terms and carefully phrasing and rephrasing the question with the desired response in mind will help clarify the task to the student. Since essay questions are to be used as a measure of complex learning outcomes, avoid starting such questions with "who," "what," "when," "where," "name," and "list." These terms tend to limit the response to knowledge outcomes. Complex achievement is most apt to be called forth by such words as "why," "describe," "explain," "compare," "relate," "contrast," "interpret," "analyze," "criticize," and "evaluate." The specific terminology to be used will, of course, be determined largely by the specific behavior described in the learning outcome to be measured.

There is no better way to check on the phrasing of an essay question than to write a model answer, or at least to formulate a mental answer, to the question. This helps the test maker detect any ambiguity in the question, aids in determining the approximate time needed by the student to develop a satisfactory answer, and provides a rough check on the mental processes required. This procedure is most feasible with the restricted-response item, the answer to which is more limited and more closely prescribed. With the extended-response form, it may be necessary to ask one or more colleagues to read the question to determine if the form and scope of the desired answer are clear.

4. Do not permit students a choice of questions unless the learning outcome requires it. In most tests of achievement, it is best to have all students answer the same questions. If they are permitted to write on only a fraction of the questions, such as three out of five, their answers cannot be evaluated on a comparative basis. Also, since the students will tend to choose those questions they are best prepared to answer, their responses will provide a sample of their achievement that is less representative than that obtained without optional questions. As we noted earlier, one of the major limitations of the essay test is the limited and unrepresentative sampling it provides. Giving students a choice among questions simply complicates the sampling problem further and introduces greater distortion into the test results.

In some situations, the use of optional questions might be defensible. For example, if the essay is to be used as a measure of writing *skill* only, some choice of topics on which to write may be desirable. This might also be the case if the essay is used to measure some aspects of creativity, or if the students have pursued individual interests through independent study. Even for these special uses, however, great caution must be exercised in the use of optional questions. The ability to organize, integrate, and express ideas is determined in part by the complexity of the content involved. Thus, an indeterminate amount of contamination can be expected when optional questions are used.

5. Provide ample time for answering and suggest a time limit in each question. Since essay questions are designed most frequently to measure intellectual skills and abilities, time must be allowed for thinking as well as for writing. Thus, generous time limits should be provided. For example, rather than expecting students to write on several essay questions during one class period, it might be better to have them focus on one or two. There seems to be a tendency for teachers to include so many questions in a single essay test that a high score is as much a measure of writing speed as of achievement. This is probably an attempt to overcome the problem of limited sampling, but it tends to be an undesirable solution. In measuring complex achievement, it would seem better to use fewer questions and to improve the sample by more frequent testing.

Informing students of the appropriate amount of time they should spend on each question will help them use their time more efficiently; ideally, it will also provide a more adequate sample of their achievement. If the length of the answer is not clearly defined by the problem, as in some extended-response questions, it might also be desirable to indicate page limits. Anything that will clarify the form and scope of the task without interfering with the measurement of the intended outcomes is likely to contribute to more effective measurement.

Rules for Scoring Essay Tests

As we noted earlier, one of the major limitations of the essay test is the subjectivity of the scoring. That is, the feelings of the scorer are likely to enter into the judgments she makes concerning the quality of the answers. This may be a personal bias toward the writer of the essay, toward certain areas of content or styles of writing, or toward shortcomings in such extraneous areas as legibility, spelling, and grammar. These biases, of course, distort the results as a measure of achievement and tend to lower their reliability.

The following rules are designed to minimize the subjectivity of the scoring and to provide as uniform a standard of scoring from one student to another as possible. These rules will be most effective, of course, when the questions have been carefully prepared in accordance with the rules for construction.

1. Evaluate answers to essay questions in terms of the learning

outcomes being measured. The essay test, like the objective test, is used to obtain evidence concerning the extent to which clearly defined learning outcomes have been achieved. Thus, the desired student behavior specified in these outcomes should serve as a guide both for constructing the questions and for evaluating the answers. If a question is designed to measure "the ability to explain cause-effect relations," for example, the answer should be evaluated in terms of how adequately the student *explains the particular cause-effect relations presented in the question.* All other factors, such as interesting but extraneous factual information, style of writing, and errors in spelling and grammar, should be ignored (to the extent possible) during the evaluation. In some cases, separate scores may be given for spelling or writing ability, but these should not be allowed to contaminate the scores that represent the degree of achievement of the intended learning outcomes.

2. ***Score restricted-response answers by the point method, using a model answer as a guide.*** Scoring with the aid of a previously prepared scoring key is possible with the restricted-response item because of the limitations placed on the answer. The procedure involves writing a model answer to each question, and determining the number of points to be assigned to it and to the parts within it. The distribution of points within an answer must, of course, take into account all scorable units indicated in the learning outcomes being measured. For example, points may be assigned to the relevance of the examples used and to the organization of the answer, as well as to the content of the answer, if these are legitimate aspects of the learning outcome. As indicated earlier, it is usually desirable to make clear to the student at the time of testing the bases on which each answer will be judged (content, organization, and so on).

3. ***Grade extended-response answers by the rating method, using defined criteria as a guide.*** Extended-response items allow so much freedom in answering that the preparation of a model answer is frequently impossible. Thus, the test maker usually *grades* each answer by judging its quality in terms of a previously determined set of criteria, rather than *scoring* it point by point with a scoring key. The criteria for judging the quality of an answer are determined by the nature of the question and thus by the learning outcomes being measured. If students were asked to "describe a complete plan for preparing an achievement test," for example, the criteria would include such things as (1) the completeness of the plan (that is, whether it included a statement of objectives, a table of specifications, the appropriate types of items, and so forth), (2) the clarity and accuracy with which each step was described,

(3) the adequacy of the justification for each step, and (4) the degree to which the various parts of the plan were properly integrated.

Typically, the criteria for evaluating an answer are used to establish about five levels of quality. Then, as the answer to a question is read, it is assigned a letter grade or a number from one to five, which designates the reader's rating. One grade may be assigned on the basis of the overall quality of the answer, or a separate judgment may be made on the basis of each criterion. The latter procedure provides the most useful information for diagnosing and improving learning, and should be used wherever possible.

More uniform standards of grading can usually be obtained by reading the answers to each question twice. During the first reading, the papers should be tentatively sorted into five piles, ranging from high to low in quality. The second reading can then serve the purpose of checking the uniformity of the answers in each pile and making any necessary shifts in rating.

4. Evaluate all of the students' answers to one question before proceeding to the next question. Scoring or grading essay tests question by question, rather than student by student, makes it possible to maintain a more uniform standard for judging the answers to each question. This procedure also helps offset the *halo effect* in grading. When all of the answers on one paper are read together, the grader's impression of the paper as a whole is apt to influence the grades he assigns to the individual answers. Grading question by question, of course, prevents the formation of this overall impression of a student's paper. Each answer is more apt to be judged on its own merits when it is read and compared with other answers to the same question, than when it is read and compared with other answers by the same student.

5. Evaluate answers to essay questions without knowing the identity of the writer. This is another attempt to control personal bias during scoring. Answers to essay questions should be evaluated in terms of what is written, not in terms of what is known about the writers from other contacts with them. The best way to prevent our prior knowledge from biasing our judgment is to evaluate each answer without knowing the identity of the writer. This can be done by having the students write their names on the back of the paper or by using code numbers in place of names.

6. Whenever possible, have two or more persons grade each answer. The best way to check on the reliability of the scoring of essay answers is to obtain two or more independent judgments. Although this may not be a feasible practice for routine classroom testing, it might be done periodically with a fellow teacher (one who is equally competent in the area).

Obtaining two or more independent ratings is especially vital if the results are to be used for important and irreversible decisions, such as the selection of students for further training or for special awards. In such cases, the pooled ratings of several competent persons may be needed to produce a level of reliability that is commensurate with the significance of the decision being made.

Additional Reading

COFFMAN, W. E., "Essay Examinations," in *Educational Measurement,* ed. R. L. Thorndike, Chap. 10. Washington, D.C.: American Council on Education, 1971. Comprehensive treatment of the construction and use of essay tests and the related research.

EBEL, R. L., *Essentials of Educational Measurement,* Chap. 6. Englewood Cliffs, N.J.: Prentice-Hall, Inc., 1972. Presents suggestions for the construction and scoring of essay questions; compares essay and objective testing.

MEHRENS, W. A., and I. J. LEHMANN, *Measurement and Evaluation in Education and Psychology,* Chap. 8. New York: Holt, Rinehart & Winston, Inc., 1973. Describes the preparation and grading of essay tests and provides examples of different types of essay questions.

PAYNE, D. A., *The Assessment of Learning: Cognitive and Affective,* Chap. 6. Lexington, Mass.: D. C. Heath and Company, 1974. Presents sample essay questions for various types of learning outcomes and describes how to construct and score essay items.

6

Constructing Performance Tests

Performance tests are useful in a variety of instructional areas. . . . These tests vary from paper-and-pencil measures of performance to samples of actual job performance. . . . As with other test types, the nature of the performance test is determined primarily by the instructional outcomes to be measured . . . and the quality of the test is enhanced by following a systematic procedure of test development.

Performance tests are concerned with skill outcomes. Skill in using processes and procedures is a desired outcome in many academic courses. For example, science courses are typically concerned with laboratory skills, mathematics courses are concerned with practical problem-solving skills, English and foreign-language courses are concerned with communication skills, and social studies courses are concerned with such skills as map and graph construction and operating effectively in a group. In addition, skill outcomes are emphasized heavily in art and music courses, industrial education, business education, agricultural education, home economics courses, and physical education. Thus, in most instructional areas performance testing provides a useful adjunct to the more commonly used paper-and-pencil measures of knowledge. Although measures of knowledge can tell us whether a student knows what to do in a particular situation, performance tests are needed to assess his actual performance skills.

Performance testing, despite the need for it, is frequently neglected in the measurement of instructional outcomes. There may be many reasons for this, but two are readily apparent. First, performance tests are more difficult to use than knowledge tests. They typically require more time to prepare and administer, and scoring them is frequently subjective and burdensome. Second, our past emphasis on norm-referenced measurement has made *indirect* measurement acceptable. Thus, if it could be shown that "knowledge about" an activity was related to actual performance of the activity, the more convenient knowledge measure could be substituted for the performance measure (since both would rank students in approximately the same order). The acceptability of such indirect measurement in education has led to an overemphasis on "knowing about" and an underemphasis on "skill in doing." The advent of criterion-referenced measurement, which emphasizes describing specifically *what each individual can and cannot do,* has put things back in proper perspective. With this form of measurement, if you want to determine what an individual "knows about" a given performance, a knowledge test is perfectly appropriate. However, if you want to describe his "proficiency in performing an activity," a performance test must be used. No matter how highly related the results of the two types of test might be, the scores on the knowledge test obviously cannot be used to describe an individual's performance skills. This emphasis on measuring each instructional outcome as directly as possible for descriptive purposes can be expected to give performance testing a much more prominent place in educational measurement.

The Nature of Performance Testing

A performance test typically falls somewhere between the usual paper-and-pencil test of cognitive outcomes and performance in the natural situation in which the learning is ultimately to be applied. It is defined by Fitzpatrick and Morrison (1971) as a test "in which some criterion situation (i.e., performance in the natural setting) is simulated to a much greater degree than is represented by the usual paper-and-pencil test." This definition makes clear that the simulation of the "real-life situation" is a matter of degree, and, thus, we can expect performance tests in any particular area to vary in the amount of "realism" that is incorporated into the test situation.

The presence of varying degrees of realism in performance testing can be illustrated by the simple example of applying arithmetic skills to the practical problem of determining correct change while shopping in a store (adapted from Fitzpatrick and Morrison, 1971). A simulation of this situation might range from the use of a story problem (low realism) to an actual purchase in a storelike situation (high realism). The various problem situations that might be contrived for this performance measure are shown in Figure 6.1. It should be noted that even though solving a story problem is relatively low in realism, it simulates the criterion situation to a greater degree than simply asking students to subtract 69 from 100. Thus, even in paper-and-pencil testing it is frequently possible to increase the degree of realism to a point where the results are useful in assessing performance outcomes.

As we shall see later, the degree of realism to be incorporated into a performance situation depends on the purpose of the instruction, the location of the performance assessment in the instructional sequence, the practical constraints operating (such as time, cost, and availability of equipment), and the nature of the particular task being measured. We shall always favor the performance measure with the highest degree of realism, but these numerous mediating factors may force us to settle for a degree of realism that falls far short of the ideal.

PROCEDURE VERSUS PRODUCT

Performance testing focuses on the procedure, the product, or some combination of the two. The nature of the performance frequently dictates where the emphasis should be placed.

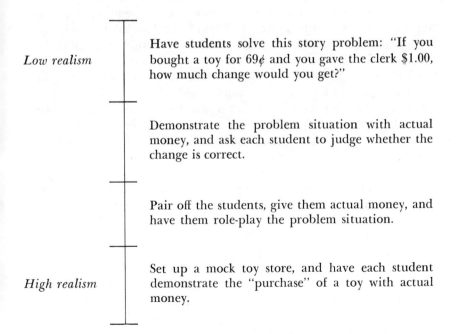

Low realism	Have students solve this story problem: "If you bought a toy for 69¢ and you gave the clerk $1.00, how much change would you get?"
	Demonstrate the problem situation with actual money, and ask each student to judge whether the change is correct.
	Pair off the students, give them actual money, and have them role-play the problem situation.
High realism	Set up a mock toy store, and have each student demonstrate the "purchase" of a toy with actual money.

Figure 6.1. *Illustration of Various Degrees of Realism in Measuring the Ability to Determine Correct Change while Making a Purchase in a Store.*

Some types of performance do not result in a tangible product. Typical examples of such performance include manipulating laboratory equipment, making a speech, playing a musical instrument, and various physical feats (for instance, swimming, dancing, and throwing a ball). Activities such as these require that the performance be evaluated in progress, special attention being paid to the constituent movements and their proper sequencing.

In some areas of performance, the product is the focus of attention and the procedure (or process) is of little or no significance. In evaluating a student's theme, drawing, or insect display, for example, the teacher is not likely to assess the procedures used by the student. This might be because various procedures could lead to an equally good product, or because the product was the result of a take-home project and the process was therefore not observable by the teacher. Also, some in-class activities are nonobservable because they involve primarily mental processes (such as problem-solving skills). In any event, in some cases only the product is evaluated. Judging the quality of the product is typically guided by specific criteria that have been prepared especially for that purpose.

In many cases, both procedure and product are important aspects of a performance. For example, skill in locating and correcting a malfunction in a television set involves following a systematic procedure (rather than using trial and error) in addition to producing a properly repaired set. Frequently, procedure is emphasized during the early stages of learning and products later, after the procedural steps have been mastered. In assessing typing skill, for example, proper use of the "touch system" would be evaluated at the beginning of instruction, but later evaluation would focus on the neatness and accuracy of the typed material and the speed with which it was produced. Similarly, in such areas as cooking, woodworking, and painting, correct procedure is likely to be stressed during the early stages of instruction and the quality of the product later. Thus, where both the procedure and the product of a performance skill are important, the degree of emphasis given to each in the assessment depends on both the skill being measured and the position of the task in the instructional sequence.

Types of Performance Tests

Performance tests can be classified in various ways. A classification system that roughly approximates the degree of realism present in the test situation includes the following types: (1) paper-and-pencil performance, (2) identification test, (3) simulated performance, and (4) work sample. Although these categories overlap to some degree, they provide a useful means of describing various approaches that might be used in measuring applied performance skills. In some cases, only one of the approaches might be used in measuring a particular skill. More commonly, two or more approaches are likely to be used at different stages of instruction.

PAPER-AND-PENCIL PERFORMANCE

A paper-and-pencil performance test differs from the more traditional paper-and-pencil test by placing greater emphasis on the application of knowledge and skill in a simulated setting. These paper-and-pencil applications might result in desired terminal learning outcomes, or they might serve as an intermediate step to performance that involves a higher degree of realism (for example, the actual use of equipment).

In a number of instances, paper-and-pencil performance can provide a product of educational significance. A course in test construction, for example, might require students to perform activities such as the following:

Construct a table of specifications for a unit of instruction.
Construct a set of test items that fits a given set of specifications.
Construct a check list for evaluating an achievement test.

The action verb *construct* is frequently used in paper-and-pencil performance testing. For instance, students might be asked to construct a weather map, bar graph, diagram of an electrical circuit, floor plan, design for an article of clothing, poem, short story, or plan for an experiment. In such cases, the paper-and-pencil product is a result of both knowledge and skill, and it provides a performance measure that is valued in its own right.

In other cases, paper-and-pencil performance might simply provide a first step toward "hands-on" performance. For example, before using a particular measuring instrument, such as a micrometer, it might be desirable to have students read various settings from pictures of the scale. Although the ability to read the scale is not a sufficient condition for accurate measurement, it is a necessary one. In this instance, paper-and-pencil testing would be favored because it is a more convenient method of testing a group of students. Using paper-and-pencil performance tests as a precursor to "hands-on" performance might be favored for other reasons. For example, if the performance is complicated and the equipment is expensive, demonstrating competence on paper-and-pencil situations could avoid subsequent accidents or damage to equipment. Similarly, in the health sciences, skill in diagnosing and prescribing for hypothetical patients could avoid later harm to real patients.

IDENTIFICATION TEST

The identification test includes a wide variety of test situations representing various degrees of realism. In some cases, a student may be asked simply to identify a tool or piece of equipment and to indicate its function. A more complex test situation might present the student with a particular performance task (for example, locating a short in an electrical circuit) and ask him to identify the tools, equipment, and procedures needed in performing the task. An even more complex type of identification test might involve listening to the operation of a malfunctioning machine (such as an automobile motor, a drill, or a lathe) and, from the sound, identifying the most probable cause of the malfunction and the proper procedure for correcting it.

Although identification tests are widely used in industrial education, they are by no means limited to that area. The biology teacher might have students identify specimens that are placed at various stations around the room, or identify the equipment and procedures needed to conduct a particular experiment. Similarly, chemistry students might be asked to identify "unknown" substances, foreign-language students to identify correct pronunciation, mathematics students to identify correct problem-solving procedures, English students to identify the "best expression" to be used in writing, and social studies students to identify various leadership roles as they are "acted out" in a group. Identifying correct procedures is also important, of course, in art, music, physical education, and such vocational areas as agriculture, business education, and home economics.

The identification test is sometimes used as an *indirect* measure of performance skill. The experienced plumber, for example, is expected to have a broader knowledge of the tools and equipment used in plumbing than the inexperienced plumber. Thus, a tool identification test might be used to eliminate the least skilled in a group of applicants for a position as plumber. More commonly, the identification test is used as an instructional device to prepare students for actual performance in real or simulated situations.

SIMULATED PERFORMANCE

Simulated performance emphasizes proper procedure. The student is typically expected to perform the same motions as those required in the actual performance of the task, but the conditions are simulated. In physical education, for example, swinging a bat at an imaginary ball, shadow boxing, and demonstrating various swimming strokes out of water are simulated performances. In science and vocational courses, laboratory work is frequently designed to simulate actual job performance. Similarly, in social studies, student role-playing of a jury trial, a city council meeting, or a job interview provides the instructor with opportunities to measure the simulated performance of an assigned task. In some cases, specially designed equipment is used for instructional and evaluative purposes. In both driver training and flight training, for example, students are frequently trained and tested on simulators. Such simulators may prevent personal injury or damage to expensive equipment during the early stages of skill development. Simulators are also used in various types of vocational training programs.

In some situations, simulated performance testing might be used as the final assessment of a performance skill. This would be the case in assessing students' laboratory performance in chemistry, for example. In many situations, however, skill in a simulated setting simply indicates readiness to attempt actual performance. The student in driver training who has demonstrated driving skill in the simulator, for example, is now ready to apply his skill in the actual operation of an automobile.

WORK SAMPLE

Of the various types of performance tests, the work sample incorporates the highest degree of realism. It requires the student to perform actual tasks that are representative of the total performance to be measured. The sample tasks typically include the most crucial elements of the total performance, and are performed under controlled conditions. In being tested for automobile driving skill, for example, the student is required to drive over a standard course that includes the most common problem situations likely to be encountered in normal driving. The student's performance on the standard course is then used as evidence of her ability to drive an automobile under typical operating conditions.

Performance tests in business education and industrial education are frequently of the work-sample type. When students are required to take and transcribe shorthand notes from dictation, type a business letter, or operate a key punch in processing business data, a work-sample assessment is being employed. Similarly, in industrial education, a work-sample approach is being used when students are required to complete a metalworking or woodworking project that includes all of the steps likely to be encountered in an actual job situation (steps such as designing, ordering materials, and constructing). Still other examples are the operation of machinery, the repair of equipment, and the performance of job-oriented laboratory tasks. The work-sample approach to assessing performance is widely used in occupations involving performance skills, and many of these situations can be duplicated in the school setting.

Steps in Constructing a Performance Test

The construction of a performance test follows somewhat the same pattern used in constructing other types of achievement tests, but involves some added complexities. The test situations can seldom be fully controlled and standardized, they typically take more time to prepare and administer, and they are frequently more difficult to score. In general, the closer the test situation approximates actual performance conditions, the greater the problems encountered in the assessment. The following procedural steps are ways of dealing with some of the common problems to be encountered in the development of performance tests. More elaborate descriptions can be found in Boyd and Shimberg (1971) and Fitzpatrick and Morrison (1971).

1. Specify the performance outcomes to be measured. If the objectives of the instruction have been prespecified the problem is simply to select those that require the use of performance tests. If the objectives have not been prespecified, they should be identified and defined for the particular areas of performance to be measured. Performance objectives commonly use action verbs such as *identify, construct,* and *demonstrate* (and their synonyms). A brief description of these verbs and some illustrative objectives are shown in Table 6.1. Most of these sample objectives would have to be defined further by a set of specific learning outcomes, following the procedure described in Chapter 2.

The specification of intended outcomes for performance testing typically includes a job or task analysis that identifies the specific activities that are most critical in successful performance. Since it is frequently impossible to measure all the procedures involved in a particular task, it is necessary to focus on a representative sample of the most crucial ones. In addition to being representative of the total performance, the selected activities should, of course, also reflect the emphasis given during instruction and should be measurable.

When the critical elements of the performance have been identified and specified, it may be desirable to set performance standards for each task. These standards indicate the minimum level of performance that is considered acceptable. They might be concerned with the accuracy of the performance (for example, "measures temperature *to the nearest two tenths of a degree*"), the speed of the performance ("locates a malfunction in electronic equipment *within three minutes*"), the proper sequencing of the steps ("adjusts a microscope *following the proper sequence of steps*), or some subjective quality ("handles tools and equipment *skillfully*"). In the last case, the subjective quality "skillfully" would have to be defined further so that observers could agree on what constitutes a minimum level of skill. The various standards set may, of course, be combined in one criterion of successful performance. In the case of the oral thermometer, for example, one criterion would typically specify both the proper procedure and the accuracy of measurement. Similarly, many performance skills combine standards of speed and accuracy (for instance, "types fifty words per minute with a maximum of two errors").

Table 6.1. *Typical Action Verbs and Illustrative Instructional Objectives for Performance Outcomes*

ACTION VERBS	ILLUSTRATIVE INSTRUCTIONAL OBJECTIVES
IDENTIFY: selects the correct objects, part of the object, procedure, or property (*typical verbs:* identify, locate, select, touch, pick up, mark, describe)	Select the proper tool. Identify the parts of a typewriter. Choose correct laboratory equipment. Select the most relevant statistical procedure. Locate an automobile malfunction. Identify a musical selection. Identify the experimental equipment needed. Identify a specimen under the microscope.
CONSTRUCT: makes a product to fit a given set of specifications (*typical verbs:* construct, assemble, build, design, draw, make, prepare)	Draw a diagram for an electrical circuit. Design a pattern for making a dress. Assemble equipment for an experimental study. Prepare a circle graph. Construct a weather map. Prepare an experimental design. Build a coffee table.
DEMONSTRATE: performs a set of operations or procedures (*typical verbs:* demonstrate, drive, measure, operate, perform, repair, set up)	Drive an automobile. Measure the volume of a liquid. Operate a filmstrip projector. Perform a modern dance step. Repair a malfunctioning TV set. Set up laboratory equipment. Demonstrate taking a patient's temperature. Demonstrate the procedure for tuning an automobile.

The importance to be assigned to each dimension of successful performance depends on the stage of instruction as well as on the nature of the performance. In assessing laboratory measurement skills, for example, accuracy might be stressed early in the instruction and concern about speed of performance might be delayed until the later stages of instruction. The particular situation in which the task is to be performed may also influence the importance of each dimension. In the measurement of typing skill, for example, speed might be stressed in the typing of routine business letters, whereas accuracy would be emphasized in the typing of statistical tables for economic reports.

2. ***Select an appropriate degree of realism.*** The degree of realism selected for a particular test situation depends on a number of factors. First, the nature of the instructional objectives must be considered. Acceptable performance in paper-and-pencil applications of skill, or in other measures with a low degree of realism, might be all that the instruction is intended to achieve. This is frequently the case with introductory courses that are to be followed by more advanced courses emphasizing applied performance. Second, the sequence of instruction within a particular course may indicate that it would be desirable to measure paper-and-pencil applications before "hands-on" performance is attempted. Locating the source of a malfunction on a diagram, for example, might precede working with actual equipment. Third, numerous practical constraints, such as time, cost, availability of equipment, and difficulties in administering and scoring, may limit the degree of realism that can be obtained. Fourth, the task itself may restrict the degree of realism in a test situation. In testing first aid skills, for example, it would be infeasible (and undesirable) to use actual patients with the wounds, broken bones, and other physical conditions needed for testing. Thus, although we should strive for as high a degree of realism as the performance outcomes dictate, it is frequently necessary to make compromises in preparing test situations.

3. ***Prepare instructions that clearly specify the test situation.*** When the test situation has been selected and the specific tasks to be performed have been identified, the next step is to prepare instructions that clearly describe the test situation. These instructions should describe the required performance and the conditions under which the performance is to be demonstrated. Instructions for a work-sample test typically include the following points:

A. purpose of the test
B. equipment and materials
C. testing procedure:

(1) condition of equipment
(2) required performance
(3) time limits (if any)

D. method of scoring

The instructions are usually written, so that all individuals are presented with the same task. In some cases the instructions are read to the examinee, and in others he reads them himself. The method of presentation depends on the complexity of the instructions and the reading ability of the examinees. In any event, the method of presentation should be specified, and should, of course, be the same for all examinees.

Carefully specifying what the examinee is to do, the conditions under which she is to perform, and the basis on which her performance is to be judged increases the likelihood that the test situation will be standard for all individuals.

4. Prepare the observational form to be used in evaluating performance. As we noted earlier, the evaluation of performance focuses on the procedure, the product, or some combination of the two. Procedures and products are frequently evaluated by some type of check list or rating scale. In addition, products are sometimes evaluated by means of a "product scale." Each of these will be described.

The *product scale* is a series of sample products that reflect different degrees of quality. A scale of this type is useful in judging the overall quality of a product and is commonly used in evaluating handwriting, works of art, and vocational projects of various types. The procedure involves selecting sample products (for instance, those of students) representing five to seven levels of quality, arranging them in order of merit, and then assigning numerical values to the levels (for example, 1 to 7). Each student's product is then rated by comparing it to the scale and determining which quality level it matches most closely. A product scale is especially useful if the quality of the product being assessed is difficult to define by a set of separate dimensions, as is the case with paintings, handicrafts, and similar works of art.

The *check list* is basically a list of measurable dimensions of a performance, or product, with a place to record a simple "yes" or "no" judgment. If a check list were used to evaluate a set of procedures, for example, the steps to be followed might be placed in sequential order on the form; the observer would then simply check whether each action was taken or not taken. Such a check list for evaluating the proper use of an oral thermometer is shown in Figure. 6.2. A check list for evaluating a product typically contains a list of the dimensions that characterize a good product (size, color, shape and so on), and a place to check whether each desired characteristic is present or absent.

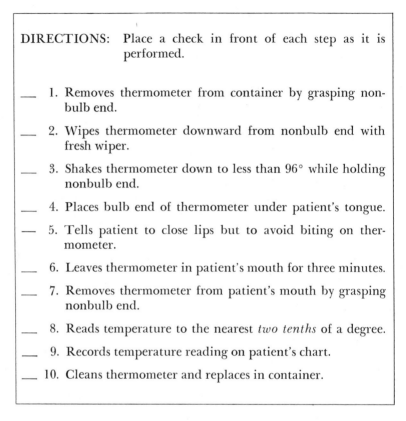

DIRECTIONS: Place a check in front of each step as it is performed.

___ 1. Removes thermometer from container by grasping nonbulb end.

___ 2. Wipes thermometer downward from nonbulb end with fresh wiper.

___ 3. Shakes thermometer down to less than 96° while holding nonbulb end.

___ 4. Places bulb end of thermometer under patient's tongue.

___ 5. Tells patient to close lips but to avoid biting on thermometer.

___ 6. Leaves thermometer in patient's mouth for three minutes.

___ 7. Removes thermometer from patient's mouth by grasping nonbulb end.

___ 8. Reads temperature to the nearest *two tenths* of a degree.

___ 9. Records temperature reading on patient's chart.

___ 10. Cleans thermometer and replaces in container.

Figure 6.2. *Check List for Evaluating the Proper Use of an Oral Thermometer.*

The *rating scale* is similar to the check list, but instead of a simple "yes" or "no" response it provides an opportunity to mark the degree to which each dimension is present. The rating scale can also be used for both procedures and products, as illustrated in the rating scale for a woodworking project shown in Figure 6.3. Although this numerical rating scale uses fixed alternatives ("outstanding," "above average," and so on), rating scales frequently use separate descriptive phrases for each of the dimensions to be rated (see Gronlund, 1976). Like the check list, the rating scale is a means of judging all students on the same set of dimensions, and it provides a convenient form on which to record the judgments.

The type of observation method used will, of course, depend mainly on the nature of the performance being evaluated.

DIRECTIONS: Rate each of the following items by circling the appropriate number. The numbers represent the following values: 5—outstanding; 4—above average; 3—average; 2—below average; 1—unsatisfactory.

Procedure Rating Scale

How effective was the student's performance in each of the following areas?

5 4 3 2 1 (a) Preparing a detailed plan for the project.

5 4 3 2 1 (b) Determining the amount of material needed.

5 4 3 2 1 (c) Selecting the proper tools.

5 4 3 2 1 (d) Following the correct procedures for each operation.

5 4 3 2 1 (e) Using tools properly and skillfully.

5 4 3 2 1 (f) Using materials without unnecessary spoilage.

5 4 3 2 1 (g) Completing the work within a reasonable amount of time.

Product Rating Scale

To what extent does the product meet the following criteria?

5 4 3 2 1 (a) The product appears neat and well constructed.

5 4 3 2 1 (b) The dimensions match the original plan.

5 4 3 2 1 (c) The finish meets specifications.

5 4 3 2 1 (d) The joints and parts fit properly.

5 4 3 2 1 (e) The materials were used effectively.

Figure 6.3. *Rating Scale for a Woodworking Project.*

Additional Reading

BALDWIN, T. S., "Evaluation of Learning in Industrial Education," in B. S. Bloom, J. T. Hastings, and G. F. Madaus, *Handbook on Formative and Summative Evaluation of Student Learning,* Chap. 23. New York: McGraw-Hill Book Company, 1971. Includes illustrative tables of specifications and test items.

BOYD, J. L., and B. SHIMBERG, *Handbook of Performance Testing: A Practical Guide for Test Makers.* Princeton, N.J.: Educational Testing Service, 1971. Describes how to prepare performance measures and presents a portfolio of sample performance tests.

FITZPATRICK, R., and E. J. MORRISON, "Performance and Product Evaluation," in *Educational Measurement* (2nd ed.), ed. R. L. Thorndike, Chap. 9. Washington, D.C.: American Council on Education, 1971. A comprehensive discussion of the principles and procedures of performance testing.

GRONLUND, N. E., *Measurement and Evaluation in Teaching* (3rd ed.), Chap. 16. New York: Macmillan Publishing Co., Inc., 1976. Describes the use of anecdotal records, rating scales, and check lists.

References Related to Applied Performance Testing. Clearinghouse for Applied Performance Testing, Northwest Regional Educational Laboratory (710 S.W. Second Avenue, Portland, Oregon, 97204). Contains approximately 500 references on applied performance testing, and information concerning the availability of each document.

7

Assembling, Administering, and Evaluating the Test

Assembling the test for use includes reviewing and editing the items. . . . arranging the items in some logical order. . . . and preparing clear directions. . . . After the test has been administered and scored, item analysis can help determine the effectiveness of each item. . . . Methods of item analysis differ for norm-referenced and criterion-referenced tests.

When constructing items for an achievement test, it is usually desirable to prepare them at least a week or two in advance. A useful practice is to prepare a few items each day while instruction is under way and the material discussed in class is still fresh in mind. In any event, early preparation makes it possible to set the items aside for a time so that they can be reviewed later with a fresh outlook. It is also desirable to prepare more items than the table of specifications calls for, since defects are likely to become apparent in some items during the later review. The extra items will make it easier for you to maintain the distribution of items reflected in the table of specifications. If you are fortunate enough to end up with more good items than the specifications call for, you can store the extra items in an item file for future use.

Each test item prepared should be written on a separate card (such as a 5-by-8 index card). This simplifies the task of reviewing the items, arranging them in the test, and filing them for future use. The index card is also a convenient place for recording item-analysis data after the effectiveness of each item has been evaluated.

Reviewing and Editing the Items

The pool of items for a particular test, after being set aside for a time, can be reviewed by the individual who constructed them or by a colleague. In either case, it is helpful for the reviewer to read and answer each item as though he were taking the test. This provides a check on the correct answer and a means of spotting any obvious defects. A more careful evaluation of the items can be made by considering them in light of each of the following questions.

1. Does each test item measure an important learning outcome included in the table of specifications? Each test item should relate to one of the cells in the table of specifications, since each item is designed to measure one aspect of the subject matter and student behavior specified in the table. If the cell to which the item refers was noted on the card at the time the item was constructed, the task is simply to read the item and recheck its appropriateness. Essay questions and complex-type objective items may, of course, have to be checked against several cells in the table. In the final analysis, each item should be related directly to the type of behavior specified by the learning outcome(s) in the table.

2. Is each item type appropriate for the particular learning outcome to be measured? Some learning outcomes can be measured by any of the common item types. In such cases, the multiple-choice item should be favored. However, if the learning outcome calls for supplying the answer, the completion or essay test must be used. If only two alternatives are plausible, the true-false item might be the most useful, and if the outcome calls for relating a series of homogeneous elements, the matching item might be more efficient. Reviewing the items provides for a second check on the appropriateness of each item type for the outcomes to be measured.

3. Does each item present a clearly formulated task? The problem presented by a test item, regardless of item type, should be so clear and unambiguous that all students understand the task they are being called upon to perform. Those who fail an item should do so only because they lack the knowledge or intellectual skill called for by the item. Although ambiguity is a major problem in test construction, it is fortunately a flaw that becomes more apparent during a follow-up review of the items.

4. Is the item stated in simple, clear language? This point is obviously related to the one above, but here we are concerned more with the appropriateness of the reading level of the item for the age group to be tested. Except for technical terms that are a necessary part of the problem, the vocabulary should be simple. Similarly, short and simple sentences are to be favored over long and complex ones. Meeting these two standards is likely to help remove ambiguity, but, equally important, they enable the poor reader to demonstrate her level of achievement more adequately. Reading ability is well worth measuring in its own right, but attempts should be made to keep it from interfering with the measurement of other learning outcomes. Ideally, the reading level of the items should be adapted to the least able reader in the group to be tested.

5. Is the item free from extraneous clues? Although we don't want a student to fail an item if he has achieved the outcome being measured, neither do we want him to answer an item correctly when he has *not* achieved the intended outcome. Thus, the review of items provides another opportunity to ferret out clues that might lead the uninformed to the correct answer. Verbal associations, grammatical inconsistencies, and other clues, which are easily overlooked during the construction of the items, frequently become obvious during review.

6. Is the difficulty of the item appropriate? As we noted earlier, the difficulty of the items in a criterion-referenced test should match the difficulty of the learning tasks set forth in the specific learning outcomes. No attempt should be made to alter item difficulty simply to obtain a spread of test scores. Since most criterion-referenced tests (for example, readiness pretests and formative tests) are used to measure student mastery, the items they contain typically have a relatively low level of difficulty. The important question here becomes, "Is the difficulty of the test item the same as that of the specified learning task?" We assume, of course, that the appropriateness of the learning task for the age group to be tested was checked at the time the list of behavioral outcomes was prepared.

In evaluating the difficulty of the items in a norm-referenced test, we shift our focus to the question, "How effectively will this item discriminate among students?" Recall that the purpose of a norm-referenced test is to obtain a dependable ranking of students, and that for us to do this we need items that discriminate. As we shall see later in this chapter, in our discussion of item analysis, test items that are answered correctly by about half of the students provide for maximum discrimination between high and low achievers. Thus, items at that level of difficulty should be favored in our review of the items to be included in a norm-referenced test. Although some easy items might be included early in the test for motivational purposes, and some difficult ones at the end to challenge the more able students, most of the items should fall near the

50 percent level of difficulty. In constructing norm-referenced tests, teachers typically err in constructing items that are too easy for the age group to be tested.

7. Is each test item independent, and are the items, as a group, free from overlapping? Knowing the answer to one item should not depend upon knowing the answer to another item. Thus, each item should be a separate scorable unit. Interlocking items are especially likely to occur when several items are based on common introductory material. A closely related problem occurs when information in one item helps the student determine the answer to another item. This is most common in tests that include both selection and supply items. Frequently, the information given in selection items is useful in answering the supply items. These defects can easily be remedied by an overall review of the items during the final selection of the items to be included in the test.

8. Do the items to be included in the test provide adequate coverage of the table of specifications? The review, elimination, and revision of test items may result in a pool of items that deviates somewhat from the table of specifications. Thus, it may be necessary to further revise some of the items or to construct new ones. In any event, the final selection of items for the test must be made in light of the table of specifications, in order to assure adequate sampling of the intended learning outcomes.

In addition to these general questions, which apply to all item types, the rules for constructing each specific type of item provide criteria for item evaluation. In the review of multiple-choice items, for example, the completeness of the problem given in the stem, the inclusion of one clearly best answer, and the plausibility of the distracters all warrant special attention. Just before reviewing a pool of items, you might find it profitable to prepare a check list of criteria based on the rules of construction for each item type.

Arranging the Items in the Test

After the final selection of the items to be assembled into a test, a decision must be made concerning the best arrangement of the items. This arrangement will vary somewhat with the type of test being prepared. The following are useful guidelines for arranging items.

1. For instructional purposes, it is usually desirable to group together items that measure the same learning outcome. The instructional uses of test results tend to be enhanced when the items are arranged according to the learning outcomes measured. Typically, all items measuring the same outcome are placed together and identified by an appropriate heading. The headings might be simply the major Taxonomy categories ("Knowledge," "Comprehension," "Application," and so forth), statements of the general instructional objectives ("Knows terms," "Knows basic principles," and so on), or statements of the specific learning outcomes ("Defines terms," "Writes a sentence using each term," and so forth). Whether to group the items by general categories or by specific outcomes depends to a large extent on the type of test being prepared. For norm-referenced tests, the general categories are usually sufficient. For criterion-referenced tests, which are used typically to measure mastery and provide feedback concerning specific learning errors, arranging the items under each specific learning outcome is favored. The inclusion of the stated headings in the test helps the teacher to identify the types of learning outcomes causing difficulty, and to plan group and individual remedial instruction.

2. Where possible, the items should be arranged so that all items of the same type are grouped together. It is desirable to group together all multiple-choice items, all short-answer items, all complex items, all essay questions, and so on. This arrangement makes it possible to provide only one set of directions for each item type. It also contributes to efficient test taking, since the student can maintain a uniform method of responding throughout each section. Finally, arranging by item type tends to simplify the scoring of the test and the analysis of the results.

If arrangement by item type conflicts with arrangement by learning outcome, grouping items by outcome should probably be favored because of the instructional value of doing so. Both types of arrangement can usually be accommodated, however, because achievement tests are typically limited to just a few item types, and because all items measuring a particular learning outcome tend to be of the same type.

3. The items should be arranged in order of increasing difficulty. It is desirable to start with easy items and to establish an order of ascending difficulty throughout the test. Doing so will have a desirable motivational effect on students and will prevent the weaker students from "bogging down" on difficult items early in the test. If the items have been grouped by learning outcome, the outcomes can be arranged in order of increasing difficulty (for example, knowledge, comprehension, and application) and the items within each section can be arranged the same way. This system will closely approximate the desired order of increasing difficulty, while maintaining the basic arrangement by learning outcome.

It is obvious that only a limited number of different methods of arranging items can be applied to the same test. However, since most tests include only a few item types, it is usually possible to honor all three of the above suggestions for item arrangement. If this is not feasible, the item arrangement that best fits the nature of the test and its intended use should be preferred. For most instructional purposes, this means favoring arrangement by learning outcome.

Preparing Directions

The directions for an achievement test should be simple and concise and yet contain information concerning each of the following: (1) purpose of the test, (2) time allowed to complete the test, (3) how to record the answers, and (4) whether to guess when in doubt about the answer. The following sample directions for a multiple-choice test cover these four points.

Example

Directions: This is a test of what you have learned during the first five weeks of the course. The results of this test will be used to clarify any points of difficulty and thus help you complete the course successfully.

There are 60 multiple-choice items, and you have one hour to complete the test.

For each item, select the answer that *best* completes the statement, or answers the question, and circle the letter of that answer.

Since your score will be the number of items answered correctly, *be sure to answer every item.*

When two or more item types are included in the same test, it is usually desirable to provide general directions for the test as a whole and specific directions for each part. When this is done, the general directions should contain the information about purpose, time allowed, and what to do about guessing, and the specific directions should describe how to record the answers for that particular part. Also, some items, such as key-type exercises, require special directions for each item.

The use of separate answer sheets requires some elaboration of the instructions for recording the answers. If students are not familiar with the use of separate answer sheets, it might also be desirable to present a sample item with the correct answer properly marked. There is a variety of separate answer sheets, and the specific instructions will, of course, have to be adapted to the particular type used. Unless machine scoring is to be used, however, a teacher-made answer sheet that simply lists the letters of the alternatives for each item is usually satisfactory:

Item	*Answer*
1.	A B C D E
2.	A B C D E
3.	A B C D E
4.	A B C D E

An answer sheet of this type should instruct the student to "put an X through the letter of the correct or best answer." Crossing out the answer is better than circling it, since an X is more visible than a circle through the holes in a scoring stencil. With this type of answer sheet, the preparation of a scoring key is simply a matter of punching out the letter of the correct answer for each item.

THE PROBLEM OF GUESSING

In our sample directions above, the students were told, "Since your score will be the number of items answered correctly, be sure to answer every item." This is an attempt to equalize the variation among students in their tendency to guess when in doubt about the answer. Such directions make it unnecessary for the instructor to correct for guessing. When students answer all items in a test, corrected and uncorrected scores rank students in exactly the same order. It is only when some items are omitted in a test that the correction makes a difference in student ranking.

There is considerable controversy concerning the issue of correcting test scores for guessing, but most of it is concerned with standardized testing. Since standardized achievement tests typically contain some material that is inappropriate for the group tested, and since all students may not have an opportunity to complete the test, directions warning them that there will be a penalty for guessing may be defensible. The aim here, of course, is to discourage students from attempting to improve their scores by guessing blindly at some of the answers. These directions do not have a uniform effect on students, however. The bold student is likely to continue to guess wildly, whereas the more hesitant student may even give up guessing on the basis of considerable knowledge.

Generally, student scores on informal achievement tests should not be corrected for guessing. The material in the test is closely related to the learning experiences of the students, and the time limits are usually liberal enough to permit the students to carefully consider all items in the test. Under these conditions, any guessing that is done is apt to be informed guessing. Although permitting such guessing may be objectionable under some conditions, guessing is quite similar to the behavior called for in making inferences, in identifying the probable causes and effects of an action, and in various decision-making aspects of problem solving. Thus, guessing is not entirely objectionable from an educational standpoint.

There may be some courses or some units within a course in which preciseness receives so much emphasis during instruction that it is desirable to stress it also during testing. In this case, "do-not-guess" instructions would be appropriate. They would also be appropriate in a speed test—that is, a test in which the students have insufficient time to consider all the items. In both instances, the students should be told that there will be a correction for guessing, and the following correction-for-guessing formula should be applied during the scoring:

$$\text{Score} = \text{Right} - \frac{\text{Wrong}}{n - 1}$$

In this formula, n equals the number of alternatives in each item. Thus, for a multiple-choice test whose items contained four alternatives, the formula would be as follows:

$$\text{Score} = \text{Right} - \frac{\text{Wrong}}{3}$$

Applying this correction-for-guessing formula involves simply counting the number of right answers and the number of wrong answers on a student's test paper and inserting these numbers in the formula. The omitted items are not counted. Thus, if a student answered 40 items correctly and 6 items incorrectly on a 50-item multiple-choice test using four alternatives, her corrected score would be computed as follows:

$$40 - \frac{6}{3} = 40 - 2 = 38$$

The assumption here is that the student guessed on 8 items and had chance success (that is, 2 right, 6 wrong). The formula simply removes those 2 right answers that can be accounted for by chance success in guessing.

Reproducing the Test

When the test is typed for reproduction, the items should be spaced on the page so that they are easy for students to read and easy for the instructor to score. If multiple-choice items are used, the alternatives should be listed underneath the stem, as in the examples presented in Chapter 3. All of the parts of an item should be on the same page. For complex-item types, however, it may be necessary to place the introductory material on a facing page, or on a separate sheet to be handed out with the test.

If the answers are to be marked on the test itself, provision should be made for recording the answers on the left side of the page. This simplifies the scoring. If separate answer sheets are to be used and the test is to be administered to more than one group of students, it is usually necessary to warn the students not to make any marks on the test booklets. It is also wise to make more copies of the test than are needed, because some students will ignore your warning.

Achievement tests for classroom use are commonly reproduced by the mimeograph, Ditto, photocopy, or photo-offset processes. Although mimeographing is satisfactory for most purposes, the use of drawings or pictures requires one of the other methods. Regardless of the method of reproduction used, the master copy should be checked carefully for item arrangement, legibility, accuracy of detail in drawings, and freedom from typographical errors.

Administering and Scoring the Test

The administration of a carefully prepared informal achievement test is largely a matter of providing proper working conditions, keeping interruptions to a minimum, and arranging enough space between students to prevent cheating. The written directions should be clear enough to make the test self-administering, but in some situations it may be desirable to give the directions orally as well. With young students, a blackboard illustration may also be useful. Above all, make certain that all the students know exactly what to do, and then provide them with the most favorable conditions in which to do it.

Scoring is facilitated if all answers are recorded on the left side of each test page, as we suggested earlier. Under this arrangement, scoring is simply a matter of marking the correct answers on a copy of the test and placing it next to the column of answers on each student's paper. If a separate answer sheet is used, it is usually better to punch out the letters of the correct answers on a copy of the answer sheet and use this as a scoring stencil. The stencil is laid over each answer sheet and the correctly marked answers appear through the holes. Where no mark appears, a red line can be drawn across the hole. This indicates to the student the correct answer for each item he missed. If machine scoring is to be used, simply scan the students' papers to make certain that only one answer was marked for each item.

Unless corrected for guessing, a student's score on an objective test is typically the number of answers marked correctly. Thus, each test item is counted as one point. Although teachers frequently desire to count some items more heavily than others, because of their importance or difficulty, such weighting of scores complicates the scoring task and seldom results in an improved measure of achievement. A better way to increase the relative weight of an area is to construct more items in that area.

Item Analysis of Norm–Referenced Tests

After a test has been administered and scored, it is usually desirable to evaluate the effectiveness of the items. This is done by studying the students' responses to each item. When formalized, the procedure is called *item analysis,* and it provides information concerning how well each item in the test functioned. Since the item-analysis procedures for norm-referenced and criterion-referenced tests differ, they will be considered separately. In this section we'll discuss norm-referenced tests (that is, tests designed to discriminate among students).

The item-analysis procedure for norm-referenced tests provides the following information:

1. The difficulty of the item.
2. The discriminating power of the item.
3. The effectiveness of each alternative.

Thus, item-analysis information can tell us if a norm-referenced item was too easy or too hard, how well it discriminated between high and low scorers on the test, and whether all of the alternatives functioned as intended. Item-analysis data also helps us detect specific technical flaws, and thus provides further information for improving test items.

Even if we have no intention of reusing the items, item analysis has several benefits. First, it provides useful information for class discussion of the test. For example, easy items can be skipped over or treated lightly, answers to difficult items can be explained more fully, and defective items can be pointed out to students rather than defended as fair. Second, item analysis provides data that helps students improve their learning. The frequency with which each incorrect answer is chosen reveals common errors and misconceptions, which provide a focus for remedial work. Third, item analysis provides insights and skills that lead to the preparation of better tests in the future.

A SIMPLIFIED ITEM-ANALYSIS PROCEDURE FOR NORM-REFERENCED TESTS

There are a number of different item-analysis procedures that might be applied to norm-referenced tests (Thorndike, 1971). For informal achievement tests used in teaching, only the simplest of procedures seems warranted. The following steps outline a simple but effective procedure. We shall use 32 test papers to illustrate the steps.

1. Arrange all 32 test papers in order from the highest score to the lowest score.

2. Select approximately one third of the papers with the highest scores and call this the *upper* group (10 papers). Select the same number of papers with the lowest scores and call this the *lower* group (10 papers). Set the middle group of papers aside (12 papers). Although these could be included in the analysis, using only the upper and lower groups simplifies the procedure.

3. For each item, count the number of students in the *upper* group who selected each alternative. Make the same count for the *lower* group.

4. Record the count from step 3 on a copy of the test, in columns to the left of the alternatives to which each count refers. The count may also be recorded on the item card or on a separate sheet, as follows:

Item 1. Alternatives	A	B*	C	D	E
Upper 10	0	6	3	1	0
Lower 10	3	2	2	3	0

* = correct answer

5. Estimate *item difficulty*, by determining the percentage of students who answered the item correctly. The simplest procedure is to base this estimate only on those students included in the item-analysis groups. Thus, sum the number of students in the upper and lower groups (10 + 10 = 20); sum the number of students who selected the correct answer

(for item 1, above, 6 + 2 = 8); and divide the first sum into the second and multiply by 100, as follows:

$$\text{Index of Item Difficulty} = \frac{8}{20} \times 100 = 40\%$$

Although our computation is based on the upper and lower groups only, it provides a close approximation of the estimate that would be obtained with the total group. Thus, it is proper to say that the index of difficulty for this item is 40 percent (for this particular group). Note that since "difficulty" refers to the *percentage answering the item correctly,* the smaller the percentage figure the more difficult the item.

The formula for computing item difficulty is as follows:

$$P = \frac{R}{T} \times 100$$

where P = the percentage who answered the item correctly; R = the number who answered the item correctly; and T = the total number who tried the item.

6. Estimate *item discriminating power,* by comparing the number of students in the upper and lower groups who answered the item correctly. Note in our sample item above that 6 students in the upper group and 2 students in the lower group selected the correct answer. This indicates *positive discrimination,* since the item differentiates between students in the same way that the total test score does. That is, students with high scores on the test (the upper group) answered the item correctly more frequently than students with low scores on the test (the lower group).

Although analysis by inspection may be all that is necessary for most purposes, an index of discrimination can easily be computed. Simply subtract the number in the lower group who answered the item correctly from the number in the upper group who answered the item correctly, and divide by the number in *each* group. For our sample item, the computation would be as follows:

$$\text{Index of Item Discriminating Power} = \frac{6 - 2}{10} = .40$$

Thus, the formula for computing item discriminating power is as follows:

$$D = \frac{R_U - R_L}{\frac{1}{2}T}$$

where D = the index of discriminating power; R_U = the number in the upper group who answered the item correctly; R_L = the number in the lower group who answered the item correctly; and $\frac{1}{2}T$ = one half of the total number of students included in the item analysis.

The discriminating power of an item is reported as a decimal fraction; maximum positive discriminating power is indicated by an index of 1.00. This is obtained *only* when all students in the upper group answer correctly and no one in the lower group does. For our illustrative upper and lower groups of 10, the computation for an item with maximum discriminating power would be as follows:

$$D = \frac{10 - 0}{10} = 1.00$$

Note that this item is at the 50 percent level of difficulty (the upper 10 answered it correctly; and the lower 10 missed it). This explains why test makers are encouraged to prepare items at the 50 percent level of difficulty for norm-referenced tests. *It is only at this level that maximum discrimination is possible.*

Zero discriminating power (.00) is obtained when an equal number of students in each group answers the item correctly. Negative discriminating power is obtained when more students in the lower group than in the upper group answer correctly. Both types of items should be removed from norm-referenced tests and then discarded or improved.

7. Determine the *effectiveness of the distracters,* by comparing the number of students in the upper and lower groups who selected each incorrect alternative. A good distracter will attract more students from the lower group than the upper group. Thus, in step 4 of our illustrative item analysis it can be seen that alternatives A and D are functioning effectively, alternate C is poor since it attracted more students from the upper group, and alternative E is completely ineffective since it attracted no one. An analysis such as this is useful in evaluating a test item, and, when combined with an inspection of the item itself, it provides helpful information for improving the item.

The above steps for analyzing items can be modified to fit particular situations. In some cases inspecting the data, rather than computing the difficulty and discriminating power, may be all that is necessary. Also, in selecting the upper and lower groups it may be desirable to use the top and bottom 25 percent if the group is large, or the upper and lower halves if the group is small. The important thing is to use a large enough fraction of the group to provide useful information. Selecting the top and bottom 27 percent of the group (as is recommended for more refined analysis) and applying other statistical refinements is seldom warranted with classroom achievement tests.

INTERPRETING ITEM-ANALYSIS DATA ON NORM-REFERENCED TESTS

Since a relatively small number of students is used when classroom tests are analyzed, item-analysis information should be interpreted with great caution. Both the difficulty and the discriminating power of an item can be expected to vary from one group to another. Thus, it doesn't seem wise to set a minimum level of discriminating power for the selection of items, or to distinguish between items on the basis of small differences in their indexes of discrimination. Other things being equal, we should favor items at the 50 percent level of difficulty and items with the highest discriminating power. However, the tentative nature of our data requires that we allow for a wide margin of error. If an item provides a positive index of discrimination, if all of the alternatives are functioning effectively, and if the item measures an educationally significant outcome, it should be retained and placed in an item file for future use.

When items are kept in an item file and reused after a period of time, it is a good practice to record the item-analysis data on the card each time the item is used. An accumulation of such data will show the variability in an item's indexes of difficulty and discriminating power and thus make the information more interpretable.

Item Analysis of Criterion-Referenced Tests

Since criterion-referenced tests are designed to describe which learning tasks a student can and cannot perform, rather than to discriminate among students, the traditional indexes of item difficulty and item discriminating power are of little value. A set of items in a criterion-referenced mastery test, for example, might be answered correctly by all students (zero discriminating power) and still be effective items. If the items closely match an important learning outcome, the results simply tell us that here is an outcome that all students have mastered. This is valuable information for describing the types of tasks students can perform, and to eliminate such items from the test would distort our descriptions of student learning.

The difficulty of an item in a criterion-referenced test is determined by the learning task it is designed to measure. If the task is easy, the item should be easy. If the task is difficult, the item should be difficult. No attempt should be made to eliminate easy items or to alter item difficulty simply to obtain a spread of test scores. Although an index of item difficulty can be computed for items in a criterion-referenced test, there is seldom a need to do so. If mastery is being measured and the instruction has been effective, criterion-referenced test items are typically answered correctly by a large percentage of the students.

ITEM-ANALYSIS PROCEDURE FOR CRITERION-REFERENCED TESTS

A basic concern in evaluating the items in a criterion-referenced mastery test is the extent to which each item is measuring the *effects of instruction.* If an item can be answered correctly by all students both *before* and *after* instruction, the item obviously is not measuring instructional effects. Similarly, if an item is answered incorrectly by all students both before and after instruction, the item is not serving its intended function. These are extreme examples, of course, but they highlight the importance of obtaining a measure of instructional effects as one basis for determining item quality.

To obtain a measure of item effectiveness based on instructional effects, the teacher must give the same test before instruction and after instruction. Effective items will be answered correctly by a larger number of students after instruction than before instruction. An index of *sensitivity to instructional effect(s)*[1] can be computed by using the following formula:

$$S = \frac{R_A - B_B}{T}$$

where R_A = the number of students answering the item correctly *after* instruction; R_B = the number answering correctly *before* instruction; and T = the total number answering the item both times. Applying this formula to an item that was answered incorrectly by all students before instruction and correctly by all students after instruction ($N = 32$), our result would be as follows:

$$S = \frac{32 - 0}{32} = 1.00$$

Thus, maximum sensitivity to instructional effects is indicated by an index of 1.00. The index of effective items will fall between .00 and 1.00, and larger positive values will indicate items with greater sensitivity to the effects of instruction.

[1] W. J. Kryspin and J. T. Feldhusen, *Developing Classroom Tests* (Minneapolis: Burgess Publishing Co., 1974) p. 166.

There are several limitations to the use of the sensitivity index. First, the teacher must give the test twice in order to compute the index. Second, a low index may be due to either an ineffective item or ineffective instruction. Third, the students' responses to the items after instruction may be influenced to some extent by their having taken the same test earlier. The last of these limitations is likely to be most serious when the instruction time is short. Despite these limitations, the sensitivity index is a useful means of evaluating the effectiveness of items in a criterion-referenced mastery test. Items are of little value in measuring the intended outcomes of instruction unless they are sensitive to instructional effects.

Additional Reading

EBEL, R. L., *Essentials of Educational Measurement,* Chaps. 9 and 14. Englewood Cliffs, N.J.: Prentice-Hall, Inc., 1972. Good descriptions of how to administer, score, and evaluate norm-referenced tests.

Educational Testing Service, Test Development Division, *Multiple-Choice Questions: A Close Look.* Princeton, N.J., 1973. Presents statistical and logical item-analysis data (norm-referenced) for a series of illustrative test items.

GRONLUND, N. E., *Measurement and Evaluation in Teaching* (3rd ed.), Chap. 11. New York: Macmillan Publishing Co., Inc., 1976. Includes descriptions of item analysis for both norm-referenced and criterion-referenced tests.

MEHRENS, W. A., and I. J. LEHMANN, *Measurement and Evaluation in Education and Psychology,* Chap. 11. New York: Holt, Rinehart & Winston, Inc., 1973. Describes how to assemble, use, and evaluate classroom tests, with emphasis on norm-referenced testing.

THORNDIKE, R. L., ed., *Educational Measurement* (2nd ed.), Chap. 5: S. Henrysson, "Gathering, Analyzing and Using Data on Test Items"; Chap. 6: R. L. Thorndike, "Reproducing the Test"; Chap. 7: W. V. Clemons, "Test Administration"; Chap. 8: F. B. Baker, "Automation of Test Scoring, Reporting and Analysis." Washington, D.C.: American Council on Education, 1971. Comprehensive treatments of the topics.

8

Simplified Methods of Interpreting Test Results

Test results can be interpreted in two basic ways. . . . Criterion-referenced interpretation describes the types of performance a student can demonstrate. . . . Norm-referenced interpretation describes how a student's performance compares with that of others. . . . Both types of interpretation are sensible . . . and each provides unique information concerning student achievement.

After an achievement test has been administered and scored, the test results must be organized in such a way that they are readily interpretable. How the results are organized and presented depends to a large extent on the type of interpretation to be made. If we are to use the test results to describe the types of tasks a student can perform (criterion-referenced interpretation), our analysis and presentation must be considerably detailed. On the other hand, if we wish simply to indicate a student's relative standing in some group (norm-referenced interpretation), a listing of total test scores may be all that is needed. Although both types of interpretation might be applied to the same test, the results are likely to be most meaningful when a test has been prepared specifically for the type of interpretation to be made. Thus, our discussion of each type of interpretation will assume that the test was designed for the method of interpretation being used.

Criterion–Referenced Interpretation

In both the construction and the interpretation of a criterion-referenced test, the focus is on the specific behavioral objectives the test is intended

Test Educational Measurement

Mastery 80% correct ***Student*** Bob Jones

OBJECTIVE	NUMBEF CORRECT	PERCENTAGE CORRECT	MASTERED (x)
1. Knows terms (20)*	18	90	X
2. Knows procedures (20)	18	90	X
3. Comprehends principles (20)	17	85	X
4. Applies principles (20)	14	60	
5. Interprets data (20)	16	80	X

* Number of items for each objective.

Figure 8.1. *Individual Report Form for a Critedion-Referenced Mastery Test.*

to measure. Each set of items is designed to measure a particular objective as directly as possible, and success on the items is interpreted with reference to the objective being measured. Thus, the results from a criterion-referenced test are typically organized in terms of the measured objectives.

Since criterion-referenced tests are used most widely in mastery testing, a performance standard for determining mastery is commonly set for each objective or each specific task. This standard might be in terms of the speed of performance (for example, "solves ten computational problems in two minutes"), the precision of the performance (for instance, "measures an obtuse angle to the nearest whole degree"), or the percentage of items answered correctly (for example, "defines 80 percent of the basic terms"). The percentage-correct score is used widely in judging whether the students have mastered the objectives, and thus in reporting the students' results on criterion-referenced tests.

A simplified individual report form using a percentage-correct standard is presented in Figure 8.1. Here the standard for mastery was set at 80, and the report shows that student Bob Jones mastered all the objectives except one. Although the setting of performance standards is somewhat arbitrary, these standards provide a useful basis for planning remedial work.[1] If a majority of students have failed to master an objective, remedial instruction can be planned for the entire group. If a smaller number of students have fallen short of mastery, individual remedial work can be prescribed.

A more detailed report form might also be useful in analyzing the results of a criterion-referenced mastery test. An item-by-item analysis, like that shown in Table 8.1, is especially useful in identifying student learning errors. By looking across the rows in the table, the teacher can evaluate the performance of each student and pinpoint her specific errors. By looking down the columns in the table, the teacher can determine the pattern of class response for each item and each cluster of items. Table 8.1 contains only a portion of an item-response chart. The complete chart would, of course, include more objectives, more items, and a larger number of students. Here, we are simply illustrating a useful format for interpreting criterion-referenced test results.

An item-response chart is especially useful in formative testing (that is, testing to improve learning), since the detailed analysis provides the type of information the instructor needs for making specific corrective prescriptions for each student. A common procedure is to key a prespecified set of corrective procedures (pages to read, programmed materials, visual aids, and so forth) to each test item or each objective.

Table 8.1. *Portion of an Item-Response Chart Showing Correct (+) and Incorrect (—) Responses to Items on a Criterion-Referenced Mastery Test*

OBJECTIVES →	KNOWS BASIC TERMS											
CONTENT AREAS →	TAXONOMY			TEST PLANNING			ITEM WRITING			ITEM ANALYSIS		
ITEM NOS. →	1	2	3	4	5	6	7	8	9	10	11	12
Jim Astor	+	+	+	+	+	+	+	+	—	+	—	—
Edna Bright	+	+	+	+	+	+	+	—	—	+	—	—
Dick Charles	+	+	—	+	+	+	—	—	+	—	+	—
Tricia Deere	+	+	+	+	+	+	+	+	+	—	+	—
Marie Lander	+	+	+	+	—	—	—	—	—	+	—	—
Erik Todd	+	+	—	—	—	—	+	—	—	—	—	—

* Either the number of items or the percentage.

[1] See N. E. Gronlund, *Preparing Criterion-Referenced Tests for Classroom Instruction* (New York: Macmillan Publishing Co., Inc., 1973), p. 12 for a procedure for setting mastery performance standards.

Assigning remedial work to an individual student is then simply a matter of checking the corrective prescriptions that match the items he answered incorrectly.

The item-response chart is also useful in checking on both the test and the instruction. If a large number of students answer an item incorrectly, it is possible either that the item is defective or that the instruction was faulty. The instructor should carefully check item 12 in Table 8.1, for example, to determine why all students answered it incorrectly. If the item is of good quality, the instruction most likely needs to be modified.

Norm–Referenced Interpretation

Since norm-referenced tests are designed to indicate how an individual's test performance compares with that of others, the interpretation of such tests is concerned with determining each individual's *relative* standing in some known group. For the classroom teacher, this typically means comparing the student with her classroom group. For purposes of comparison it is common to use the student's total raw score on the test, or some score that has been derived from the raw score. Our discussion here will be confined to a few simplified methods of treating raw scores and to the computation of *stanines,* a derived score that is easily computed and widely used with classroom tests. For a more comprehensive, but simplified, treatment of the topic, see the brief book by Townsend and Burke (1975).

SIMPLE RANKING OF RAW SCORES

A common method of presenting the scores on a norm-referenced test to the class is to simply list the scores on the blackboard. This is typically done by ranking the scores from high to low and making a frequency count to show the number (N) of students earning each score. A sample frequency distribution of this type is presented in Table 8.2. This table shows a distribution of scores for 30 students ($N = 30$) on a test containing 40 objective items. By looking at a simple ranking of raw scores, like that in Table 8.2, each student can easily determine his relative standing in the group.

STATISTICS FOR DESCRIBING A SET OF SCORES

For some purposes, it is desirable to describe a set of scores in briefer form than that of a total ranking. This is typically done by computing two measures: (1) the average score, or measure of *central tendency,* and (2) the spread of scores, or measure of *variability.*

Statisticians frown on the use of the term "average" in describing test scores because there are a number of different types of average. It is more precise to use the term that denotes the particular average being used. The three common types of averages are (1) the *median,* or counting average, which is determined by arranging the scores in order of size and counting up to the midpoint of the series of scores; (2) the *mean,* or arithmetic average, which is determined by adding all of the scores in a set and dividing the sum by the total number of scores, and (3) the *mode,* the score that occurs most frequently, which is determined simply by inspecting the frequency of each score. Of these types, the median (commonly represented by *Mdn)* and the mean (commonly represented by *M* or $\overline{X}$) are used most frequently to describe the central tendency of a set of scores.

The spread, or variability, of a set of scores can be described in a number of different ways. Two of the more useful for describing test scores are (1) the *range,* which is simply the interval between the highest and lowest scores, and (2) the *standard deviation,* which is essentially an average of the degree to which the scores in a set deviate from the mean. The meaning of the standard deviation is grasped most easily by noting that a distance of one standard deviation above the mean and one standard deviation below the mean encompasses approximately the middle two thirds of the scores (68 percent in a normal distribution). Thus, like the range for a set of scores, a large standard deviation indicates a big spread of scores (or great variability) and a smaller standard deviation indicates a smaller spread of scores (or less variability).

The standard deviation (*SD* or *s*) is an important and widely applicable statistic in testing. In addition to its use in describing the spread of scores in a group, it also serves as a basis for computing reliability coefficients, the standard error of measurement, and standard scores.

In describing test scores, the range may be used with the median or the mean. The standard deviation is used only with the mean.

DETERMINING THE MEDIAN AND RANGE

The simplest method of describing test scores is to use the median and the range.[2] These two measures are used when the group is small and

[2] The *quartile deviation* can be used in place of the range but this is seldom done in describing test scores for classroom use.

Table 8.2. *Frequency Distribution of Test Scores for an Objective Test of 40 Items*

TEST SCORE	FREQUENCY
38	1
37	1
36	0
35	2
34	1
33	2
32	3
31	2
30	1
29	4 ← Median
28	2
27	2
26	2
25	3
24	1
23	0
22	1
21	1
20	0
19	1
	$N = 30$

there is no need to compute further statistics. Thus, they might be used during class discussion to help students better understand their position in the group; and then they can be filed or discarded.

The first step is to rank the test scores, as shown in Table 8.2. The median is then determined, by locating the midpoint of the set of scores. This can be done by counting up from the bottom, in the frequency column, to the point midway between the fifteenth and sixteenth scores (15 scores are above this point and 15 below). In this case the midpoint falls at score 29. Had the midpoint fallen between scores 29 and 30, we would use 29.5 for the median. With an odd number of scores, the median always falls on an actual score, because there is an equal number of scores above and below the middle score.[3]

The range of scores is determined by subtracting the lowest score from the highest score (sometimes 1 is added to the result). The range of our sample set of 30 student scores is 19 (38 − 19). Thus, this set of scores can be described as having a median of 29 and a range of 19. As we noted earlier, these are terminal values: they are suitable for describing the

[3] More precise values for the median can be obtained with formulas found in standard statistics books, but these estimates are sufficiently precise for most classroom uses.

scores of a small group of students, such as our group of 30, but they are not useful in computing further statistics.

DETERMINING THE MEAN AND STANDARD DEVIATION

The mean and standard deviation are based on the value of each score in the set and thus provide more stable measures than those obtained by counting. In addition, these statistics are used in computing a number of other statistics that are useful in testing (such as reliability measures and standard scores). For these reasons, the mean and standard deviation are the preferred measures for analyzing and describing test scores.

The mean is obtained by adding all the scores in the group and dividing by the number of scores. From Table 8.2, we can determine that the sum of the 30 student scores is 872; when this sum is divided by 30, a mean of 29.07 is obtained.

The simplest means of estimating the standard deviation is one presented in a bulletin by Diederich (1973). This procedure involves simply subtracting the sum of the bottom sixth of the scores from the sum of the top sixth and dividing by half the number of students in the group. Thus,

$$\text{Standard deviation } (s) = \frac{\text{Sum of high sixth} - \text{Sum of low sixth}}{\text{Half the number of students}}$$

In applying this formula to the set of scores in Table 8.2, we would add the top five scores (one sixth of 30) to obtain 179, add the bottom five scores to obtain 111, subtract the latter sum from the former, and divide the result by 15 (one half of 30):

$$s = \frac{179 - 111}{15} = 4.53$$

Thus, our sample set of scores can be described as having a mean of 29 (rounded) and a standard deviation of 4.5 (rounded). Were this a normal distribution, we would expect about two thirds of the scores to fall between 24.5 (29 − 4.5) and 33.5 (29 + 4.5). Seventy percent of the scores in Table 8.2 fall within this range. With a small number of scores, such as our sample group of 30, a perfectly normal distribution of scores is not to be expected. The distribution of a small number of test scores is frequently close enough to a normal distribution, however, that the standard deviation can be used meaningfully to describe the spread of scores in the group.

USING THE STANINE SYSTEM OF STANDARD SCORES

In teaching, we frequently like to compare a student's relative achievement on different tests, or compare her standing on a test with her standing on some other measure of achievement (for instance, an assessment of theme writing or a rating of laboratory performance). Similarly, in assigning and reporting grades, we need some means of combining such diverse elements as test scores, ratings, and evaluations of various types of written work into a composite score or final grade. This task is usually complicated by our desire to weight some elements more than others. These and similar problems require that we make all the data comparable by converting them to a common scale.

A number of different systems of standard scores are useful for comparing or combining test scores and other types of data. The system that is simplest to understand and use is the *stanine* (pronounced *stay-nine*) system. This system is not only useful for classroom achievement tests, but is also used widely with standardized tests of all types. This is an additional advantage, in that a student's scores on classroom tests can be compared readily with her standing on standardized tests of aptitude and achievement.

The nature of the stanine system. The stanine scale is a system of standard scores that divides the distribution of raw scores into nine parts (the term *stanine* was derived from *standard nines*). The highest stanine score is 9, the lowest is 1, and stanine 5 is located precisely in the center of the distribution. Each stanine, except 1 and 9, includes a band of raw scores one-half of a standard deviation wide. Thus, stanines are normally distributed standard scores with a mean of 5 and a standard deviation of 2. The percentage of a group that falls within each stanine in a normal distribution is as follows:

Stanine	1	2	3	4	5	6	7	8	9
Percentage	4	7	12	17	20	17	12	7	4

One of the greatest advantages of stanines is that we can apply them to any type of data that approximate a normal distribution and that can be ranked from high to low. We simply assign the top 4 percent of the students a stanine of 9, the next 7 percent a stanine of 8, and so on. To simplify this process, we can use tables such as Table 8.3 to determine the *number* of individuals in a group who should be assigned each stanine.

Table 8.3. *Number of Individuals to be Assigned Each Stanine Score*

	STANINES								
	1	2	3	4	5	6	7	8	9
SIZE OF GROUP	NUMBER OF INDIVIDUALS RECEIVING STANINE SCORE								
20	1	1	2	4	4	4	2	1	1
21	1	1	2	4	5	4	2	1	1
22	1	2	2	4	4	4	2	2	1
23	1	2	2	4	5	4	2	2	1
24	1	2	3	4	4	4	3	2	1
25	1	2	3	4	5	4	3	2	1
26	1	2	3	4	6	4	3	2	1
27	1	2	3	5	5	5	3	2	1
28	1	2	3	5	6	5	3	2	1
29	1	2	4	5	5	5	4	2	1
30	1	2	4	5	6	5	4	2	1
31	1	2	4	5	7	5	4	2	1
32	1	2	4	6	6	6	4	2	1
33	1	2	4	6	7	6	4	2	1
34	1	3	4	6	6	6	4	3	1
35	1	3	4	6	7	6	4	3	1
36	1	3	4	6	8	6	4	3	1
37	2	3	4	6	7	6	4	3	2
38	1	3	5	6	8	6	5	3	1
39	1	3	5	7	7	7	5	3	1
40	1	3	5	7	8	7	5	3	1
41	1	3	5	7	9	7	5	3	1
42	2	3	5	7	8	7	5	3	2
43	2	3	5	7	9	7	5	3	2
44	2	3	5	8	8	8	5	3	2
45	2	3	5	8	9	8	5	3	2
46	2	3	5	8	10	8	5	3	2
47	2	3	6	8	9	8	6	3	2
48	2	3	6	8	10	8	6	3	2
49	2	4	6	8	9	8	6	4	2
50	2	3	6	9	10	9	6	3	2
51	2	3	6	9	11	9	6	3	2
52	2	4	6	9	10	9	6	4	2
53	2	4	6	9	11	9	6	4	2
54	2	4	7	9	10	9	7	4	2
55	2	4	7	9	11	9	7	4	2
56	2	4	7	9	12	9	7	4	2
57	2	4	7	10	11	10	7	4	2
58	2	4	7	10	12	10	7	4	2
59	3	4	7	10	11	10	7	4	3
60	3	4	7	10	12	10	7	4	3

Note: If more than 60 students are in the group, see Gronlund (1976).

To use Table 8.3, all we need to do is enter the table with the size of the group with which we are working and, reading across the table, note the number of students who should be assigned each stanine score. For example, with a group of 30 students, 1 student would be assigned a stanine score of 1, 2 students a stanine score of 2, 4 students a stanine score of 3, and so on.

When raw scores are converted to stanines, they are in effect placed on a standard scale. This provides uniform meaning from one part of the scale to another and from one set of measures to another. Thus, the difference between a stanine of 7 and a stanine of 8 is the same as the difference between a stanine of 4 and a stanine of 5 or a stanine of 2 and a stanine of 3. This standard scale also makes it possible to compare relative standing on diverse types of measures. Whe stanines are all *based on the same group of students,* a particular stanine score refers to the same position in the group whether we are talking about scores on objective tests, essay ratings, oral reports, or a term paper. Thus, a stanine of 7 on each of these various measures would indicate the same distance above average. The simplicity of the system resides in the fact that we have standard units that can be expressed by a single digit. Since the mean score is always 5, relative standing within a set of scores and comparative standing on different sets of scores can be quickly perceived.

Probably the most useful function stanines serve is in the weighting and combining of diverse types of data for the purpose of obtaining a composite score, as in the determination of school marks. For example, let's assume that we have stanine scores for a mid-semester examination, laboratory work, and a final examination, and that we wish to give the first two equal weight and the final examination twice as much weight as either of the other two. For a student with the following stanine scores, then, our computation of a composite score would be as follows:

	STANINE		WEIGHT	WEIGHTED SCORE
Mid-semester examination	6	×	1	6
Laboratory work	4	×	1	4
Final examination	8	×	2	16
				Total = 26

$$\text{Composite score} = \frac{26}{4} = 6.5$$

If composite scores were computed, as above, for each student in the group, these scores would provide a basis for ranking the students from high to low in terms of overall achievement. If final grades were to be assigned, the instructor would then simply decide how many students should be given As, how many Bs, how many Cs, and so on. Note that the composite score is not a stanine, and that it does not tell us what grade should be assigned. It simply provides a ranking of students that accurately reflects the emphasis we wanted to give to each measure of achievement. The percentage of students to be assigned each letter grade is not a statistical decision, but rather one that must be based on the educational level of the group, the ability of the students, the nature of the instruction, and the purposes to be served by the grades (Gronlund, 1974).

Assigning stanines to test scores. If we wish to assign stanines to data that are in rank order and there are no ties in rank, we simply go down the ranked list and assign stanines in accordance with the distribution of stanine scores indicated in Table 8.3. When assigning stanines to test scores, however, we frequently have several students with the same raw score. Tie scores force us to deviate somewhat from the distribution in Table 8.3, since obviously *all students with the same raw score must be assigned the same stanine.* In assigning stanines to test scores, then, we try to approximate the theoretical distribution in Table 8.3 as closely as possible.

The steps to be followed in assigning stanines to test scores are listed below and illustrated by the data in Table 8.4. Note that the scores described in Table 8.4 are the same 30 test scores that were used earlier in this chapter.

1. Make a frequency distribution of scores: list every score from highest to lowest, and record in the frequency column the number of students who obtained each score (total number = 30 in Table 8.4).

2. In the frequency column, count up from the bottom to the midpoint (median) of the set of scores (median = 29 in Table 8.4).

3. Enter the stanine table (Table 8.3), for a group size of 30 and determine the number of individuals to which a stanine of 5 should be assigned (6 individuals). By going above and below the median, mark off as close to this number of scores (6) as possible (in Table 8.4, 7 scores were included to keep stanine 5 centered).

4. By working up and down from stanine 5, assign raw scores to each stanine level so as to approximate the theoretical grouping (obtained from Table 8.3 and shown in Table 8.4) as closely as possible. If raw scores can be assigned to either of two stanines equally well, assign them to the stanine nearest the mean. In Table 8.4, for example, note that the two raw scores of 35 could be assigned to stanine 7 or stanine 8. They are assigned to stanine 7 in accordance with our rule.

5. When a tentative assignment has been completed, recheck to be

Table 8.4. *Assigning Stanines to a Frequency Distribution of Test Scores*

STANINE	TEST SCORE	FREQUENCY	ACTUAL GROUPING	THEORETICAL GROUPING
9	38	1	1	1
8	37	1	1	2
	36	0		
7	35	2	5	4
	34	1		
	33	2		
6	32	3	5	5
	31	2		
5	30	1	7	6
	29	4		
	28	2		
4	27	2	4	5
	26	2		
3	25	3	4	4
	24	1		
	23	0		
2	22	1	2	2
	21	1		
1	20	0	1	1
	19	1		
		$N = 30$		

certain that the actual grouping is as close to the theoretical distribution as possible. Then draw lines across the page, as shown in Table 8.4, and group the raw scores by stanine level.

Additional Reading

DIEDERICH, P. B., *Short-Cut Statistics for Teacher-Made Tests.* Princeton, N.J.: Educational Testing Service, 1973. Presents simplified procedures for using statistics with norm-referenced scores.

EBEL, R. L., *Essentials of Educational Measurement,* Chap. 11. Englewood Cliffs, N.J.: Prentice-Hall, Inc., 1972. Good treatment of statistics for norm-referenced scores.

GRONLUND, N. E., *Improving Marking and Reporting in Classroom Instruction.* New York: Macmillan Publishing Co., Inc., 1974. Describes criterion-referenced and norm-referenced marking and reporting.

———, *Measurement and Evaluation in Teaching* (3rd ed.), Appendix A. New York: Macmillan Publishing Co., Inc., 1976. Simplified treatment of statistical methods that are useful in analyzing norm-referenced test scores.

LINDVALL, C. M., and A. J. NITKO, *Measuring Pupil Achievement and Aptitude* (2nd ed.), Chap. 5. New York: Harcourt Brace Jovanovich, Inc., 1975. Covers both criterion-referenced and norm-referenced interpretation of test scores.

LYMAN, H. B., *Test Scores and What They Mean* (2nd ed.). Englewood Cliffs, N.J.: Prentice-Hall, Inc., 1971. Comprehensive and clear treatment of norm-referenced scores.

TOWNSEND, E. A., and P. J. BURKE, *Using Statistics in Classroom Instruction.* New York: Macmillan Publishing Co., Inc., 1975. A brief how-to-do-it book (94 pages) containing numerous illustrations and exercises on the analysis of norm-referenced scores.

9

Validity and Reliability

Validity refers to the appropriateness of the interpretations of test results. . . . Reliability refers to the consistency of test results. . . . Both are important concepts in the development and use of achievement tests. . . . Validity is most important . . . but reliability provides the consistency that makes validity possible, and indicates the confidence to be placed in test interpretations.

The two most important qualities to consider in the preparation and use of achievement tests are *validity* and *reliability*. Both are essential to effective testing and should be understood by anyone working with tests. Even though it is frequently unnecessary to make elaborate validation and reliability studies of informal achievement tests, a clear grasp of these concepts will contribute to skill in test construction and test interpretation.

Methods of Determining Validity

In a very general sense, validity is concerned with the extent to which test results serve their intended use. For example, test results might be used to describe the types of performance an individual can demonstrate, or to predict an individual's probable success in some future activity. Questions of validity in the first instance are concerned with what behavioral responses are being measured by the test, and in the second instance with how closely the scores on the test are related to some other valued performance. Thus, "questions of validity are questions of what may properly be inferred from a test score" (American Psychological Association, 1974). Since test results may serve many different uses, there are many different types of inferences that might be drawn from test scores. Specifically, then, validity refers to the appropriateness of the interpretations of test results (typically with regard to some practical use of the test results).

The concept of validity, as used in testing, can be clarified further by noting the following general points:

1. Validity refers to the *interpretation of test results* (not to the test itself).
2. Validity is *inferred* from available evidence (not measured).
3. Validity is *specific* to a particular use (selection, placement, evaluation of learning, and so forth).
4. Validity is expressed by *degree* (for example, high, moderate, or low).

A standard and widely adopted classification system (American Psychological Association, 1974) divides validity into the following basic types: (1) *content* validity, (2) *criterion-related* validities (*predictive* and *concurrent*), and (3) *construct* validity. The type of question to be answered by each is shown in Table 9.1.

Each of these basic types of validity will be discussed in turn. Although our primary concern in constructing and using achievement tests is with content validity, the other types of validity have some relevance for achievement testing. In addition, an understanding of the various types of validity is essential for an adequate comprehension of the literature on testing.

Table 9.1. *Basic Types of Validity*

TYPE	QUESTION TO BE ANSWERED
Content validity	How adequately does the test content sample the larger universe of situations it represents?
Criterion-related validities	How well does test performance predict future performance (predictive validity) or estimate present standing (concurrent validity) on some other valued measure called a *criterion?*
Construct validity	How well can test performance be explained in terms of psychological attributes?

CONTENT VALIDITY

We are interested in content validity when we want to use test performance as evidence of performance in a larger universe of situations. Let's assume, for example, that we have a list of 500 words that we expect our students to be able to spell correctly at the end of the school year. To test their spelling ability, we might give them a 50-word spelling test. Their performance on these words is important only insofar as it provides evidence of their ability to spell the 500 words. Thus, our spelling test would have content validity to the degree to which it provided an adequate sample of the 500 words it represented. If we selected only easy words, only difficult words, or only words that represented certain types of common spelling errors, our test would tend to have low content validity. If we selected a balanced sample of words that took these and similar factors into account, our test would tend to have high content validity.

It should be clear from this discussion that the key element in content validity is the adequacy of the *sampling*. A test is always a sample of the many questions that could be asked. Content validity is a matter of determining whether the sample is representative of the larger universe it is supposed to represent.

Content validity is especially important in achievement testing. Here we are interested in how well the test measures the subject matter topics and learning outcomes covered during the instructional period. We can build a test that has high content validity by (1) identifying the subject-matter topics and behavioral outcomes to be measured, (2) building a table of specification, which specifies the sample of items to be used, and (3) constructing a test that closely fits the table of specifications. These are the best procedures we have for ensuring the measurement of a representative sample of both the subject matter and the behavioral outcomes under consideration—in short, for ensuring high content validity. Note that these three procedures are the same ones we have described in considerable detail in earlier chapters. Thus, we have been concerned with content validity throughout this entire book, even though we have not identified it as such.

The makers of standardized tests follow these same systematic procedures in building achievement tests, but the content and behavioral outcomes included in the table of specifications are based more broadly. Typically, they are based on the leading textbooks and the recommendations of various experts in the area being covered by the test. Thus, a standardized achievement test may have high content validity in a general sense, in that it represents the common content and objectives in the area, and still have low content validity in a particular school situation.

To determine whether a standardized achievement test is valid for use in a particular classroom, we must evaluate the test items in light of the content and objectives that are emphasized in the instruction.

Content validity is of major concern in achievement testing, and it is important to have in both criterion-referenced and norm-referenced tests. Although these two test types are used for different purposes, both require generalizing from the test behavior to the larger domain of behavior that the test is designed to measure. Thus, how adequately the test has sampled the intended outcomes is a vital question. Unfortunately, there is no simple statistical procedure for determining this adequacy. Whether a test is constructed or selected, the evaluation of content validity is a rather long, involved process based on careful logical analysis.

CRITERION-RELATED VALIDITIES

There are two types of criterion-related validity. The first is concerned with the use of test performance to predict future performance on some other valued measure called a *criterion*. For example, we might use scholastic aptitude test scores to predict course grades (the criterion). For obvious reasons, this type of validity is called *predictive* validity. The second type of criterion-related validity is concerned with the use of test performance to estimate current performance on some criterion. For instance, we might want to use a test of study skills to estimate what the outcome would be of a careful observation of students in an actual study situation (the criterion). Since with this procedure both measures (test and criterion) are obtained at approximately the same time, this type of validity is called *concurrent* validity.

Although the value of establishing predictive validity is rather obvious, a question might be raised concerning the purpose of concurrent validity. Why would anyone want to use test scores to estimate performance on some other measure that is to be obtained at the same time? There are at least three good reasons for doing this. First, we may want to check the results of a newly constructed test against some existing test that is known to be valid. Second, we may want to substitute a brief, simple testing procedure for a more complex and time-consuming measure. For example, our test of study skills might be substituted for an elaborate rating system if it provided a satisfactory estimate of study performance. Third, we may want to determine whether a testing procedure has *potential* as a predictive instrument. If a test provides an unsatisfactory estimate of current performance, it certainly cannot be expected to predict future performance on the same measure. On the other hand, a satisfactory estimate of present performance would indicate that the test *may* be useful (but less accurate) in predicting future performance as well. This would inform us that a predictive study would be worth doing.

The key element in both types of criterion-related validity is the *degree of relationship* between the two sets of measures: (1) the test scores, and (2) the criterion to be predicted or estimated. This relationship is typically expressed by means of a correlation coefficient or an expectancy table.

Correlation coefficients. Although the computation of correlation coefficients is beyond the scope of this book, the concept of correlation can easily be grasped. A correlation coefficient (r) simply indicates the degree of relationship between two sets of measures. A *positive* relationship is indicated when high scores on one measure are accompanied by high scores on the other; low scores on the two measures are associated similarly. A *negative* relationship is indicated when high scores on one measure are accompanied by low scores on the other measure. The extreme degrees of relationship it is possible to obtain between two sets of scores are indicated by the following values:

1.00 = perfect positive relationship
.00 = no relationship
−1.00 = perfect negative relationship

When a correlation coefficient is used to express the degree of relationship between a set of test scores and some criterion measure, it is called a *validity coefficient*. For example, a validity coefficient of 1.00 applied to the relationship between a set of aptitude-test scores (the predictor) and a set of achievement-test scores (the criterion) would indicate that each individual in the group had exactly the same relative standing on both measures, and would thereby provide a perfect prediction from the aptitude scores to the achievement scores. Most validity coefficients are, of course, smaller than this, but the extreme positive relationship provides a useful bench mark for evaluating validity coefficients. The closer the validity coefficient approaches 1.00, the higher the criterion-related validity and, thus, the more accurate our predictions of each individual's success on the criterion will be.

A more realistic procedure for evaluating a validity coefficient is to compare it to the validity coefficients that are *typically* obtained when the two measures are correlated. For example, a validity coefficient of .40 between a set of aptitude test scores and achievement test scores would be considered small because we typically obtain coefficients in the .50-to-.70

range for these two measures. Thus, validity coefficients must be judged on a relative basis, the larger coefficients being favored. To use validity coefficients effectively, one must, of course, become familiar with the size of the validity coefficients that are typically obtained between various pairs of measures.

Since we need score variability in order to compute validity coefficients, this method of reporting criterion-related validity is used primarily with norm-referenced tests. Computing validity coefficients for criterion-referenced mastery tests is likely to produce distorted results because score variability on such tests is typically quite small. It might even be nonexistent (for example, all students might obtain perfect scores), in which case a validity coefficient could not be computed.

Expectancy table. The expectancy table is a simple and practical means of expressing criterion-related validity, and is especially useful for making predictions from test scores. The expectancy table is simply a twofold chart with the test scores (the predictor) arranged in categories down the left side of the table and the measure to be predicted (the criterion) arranged in categories across the top of the table. For each category of scores on the *predictor,* the table indicates the percentage of individuals who fall within each category of the *criterion.* An example of an expectancy table is presented in Table 9.2.

Note in Table 9.2 that of those students who were in the above-average group (stanines 7, 8, and 9) on the test scores, 43 percent received a grade of A, 43 percent a B, and 14 percent a C. Although these percentages are based on this particular group, it is possible to use them to predict the future performance of other students in this science course. Thus, if a student falls in the above-average group on this scholastic-aptitude test, we might predict that she has 43 chances out of 100 of

Table 9.2. *Expectancy Table Showing the Relation Between Scholastic-Aptitude Scores and Course Grades for 30 Students in a Science Course*

GROUPED SCHOLASTIC APTITUDE SCORES (STANINES)	PERCENTAGE IN EACH SCORE CATEGORY RECEIVING EACH GRADE				
	E	D	C	B	A
Above Average (7, 8, 9)			14	43	43
Average (4, 5, 6)		19	37	25	19
Below Average (1, 2, 3)	57	29	14		

earning an A, 43 chances out of 100 of earning a B, and 14 chances out of 100 of earning a C in this particular science course. Such predictions are highly tentative, of course, due to the small number of students on which this expectancy table was built. Teachers can construct more dependable tables by accumulating data from several classes over a period of time.

Expectancy tables can be used to show the relationship between any two measures. Constructing the table is simply a matter of (1) grouping the scores on each measure into a series of categories (any number of them), (2) placing the two sets of categories on a twofold chart, (3) tabulating the number of students who fall into each position in the table (based on the student's standing on both measures), and (4) converting these numbers to percentages (of the total number in that row). Thus, the expectancy table is a quick, easy means of expressing the relationship between sets of scores.

The expectancy table can be used with criterion-referenced as well as norm-referenced tests. In predicting success on a criterion-referenced mastery test, for example, we could simply limit the categories across the top of the table to two—*mastery* and *nonmastery*. The table would then show, for each score level on the predictor, what proportion of the students had demonstrated mastery on the criterion.

CONSTRUCT VALIDITY

We are interested in construct validity when we want to use an individual's test performance as a basis for inferring his possession of certain psychological traits or qualities. For example, instead of talking about an individual's scores on test X, we want to talk about the individual's intelligence, reasoning ability, or mechanical aptitude. These are all hypothetical qualities, or *constructs,* that we assume exist in order that we may account for behavior in many different specific situations. To describe a person as being highly intelligent, for example, is useful because that term carries with it a series of associated meanings that indicate what his behavior is likely to be under various conditions. Before we can interpret test scores in terms of these broad behavioral descriptions, however, we must first establish that the constructs that are presumed to be reflected in the test scores actually do account for differences in test performance. This process is called *construct validation.*

The aim in determining construct validity is to identify all the factors that influence test performance and to determine the degree of influence of each. The process includes the following steps: (1) identifying the constructs that might account for test performance, (2) formulating testable hypotheses from the theory surrounding each construct, and (3) gathering data to test these hypotheses (Cronbach, 1971). For example, to check on the claim that a test measures mathematical reasoning ability, we would state and test a series of hypotheses that indicate how the test scores should vary if test performance reflects mathematical reasoning. These hypotheses might be stated in harmony with any of the following general types of evidence (Helmstadter, 1964):

1. Differences between groups: we might predict, for example, that boys would have higher scores on a test of mathematical reasoning than girls.
2. Changes in performance with training: we might predict fairly stable scores on a series of mathematical reasoning tests; for other types of tests we might predict great change.
3. Correlations with other tests: we might predict high correlations between the test in question and other mathematical reasoning tests; we might also predict low correlations between this test and tests on subjects known to have little relationship with mathematical reasoning.
4. Internal consistency: we might predict high intercorrelations among the items of this test because they all supposedly measure one trait—mathematical reasoning.
5. Study of the test-taking process: we could have students "think aloud" as they take the test and analyze the mental process that they use to obtain the answers.

As you can see from this discussion, no single type of evidence is satisfactory for determining construct validity. What we do is make predictions that are in harmony with the theory underlying the particular construct and test them one by one. If the data are in harmony with our predictions, they support the validity of our interpretations of the scores as a measure of the construct. If the data are contrary to our predictions, we must revise the test interpretation, reformulate the theory underlying the construct, or improve the experimental design used to obtain the data.

Since test scores cannot be interpreted as a measure of only one construct, the process of construct validation typically includes a study of the influence of several factors. We might, for example, ask to what extent the scores on our mathematical reasoning test are influenced by reading comprehension, computational skill, and speed. Each of these factors would require a further study. The key element in construct validity, then, is the *experimental verification* of the test interpretations we propose to make. This involves a wide variety of procedures and many different types of evidence. As evidence accumulates concerning the meaning of the test scores, our interpretations are enriched and we are able to make them with greater confidence.

Although construct validity is applicable to both norm-referenced and criterion-referenced tests, evidence in the latter case would, of necessity, be less dependent on statistical measures requiring score variability.

Methods of Determining Reliability

Reliability refers to the *consistency* of test scores—that is, to how consistent they are from one measurement to another. Because of the ever present errors of measurement, we can expect a certain amount of variation in test performance from one time to another, from one sample of items to another, and from one part of the test to another. Reliability measures provide an estimate of how much variation we might expect under different conditions. The reliability of test scores is typically reported by means of a *reliability coefficient* or the *standard error of measurement* that is derived from it. Since both methods of estimating reliability require score variability, the procedures to be discussed are useful primarily with norm-referenced tests.

As we noted earlier, a correlation coefficient expressing the relationship between a set of test scores and a criterion measure is called a validity coefficient. A reliability coefficient is also a correlation coefficient, but it indicates the correlation between two sets of measurements taken from the same procedure. We may, for example, administer the same test twice to a group, with an intervening time interval (*test-retest* method); administer two equivalent forms of the test in close succession (*equivalent-forms* method); administer two equivalent forms of the test with an intervening time interval (*test-retest* with *equivalent-forms* method); or administer the test once and compute the consistency of the responses within the test (*internal-consistency* method). Each of these methods of obtaining reliability coefficients provides a different type of information (American Psychological Association, 1974). Thus, reliability coefficients obtained with the different procedures are not interchangeable. Before deciding on the procedure to be used, we must determine what type of reliability evidence we are seeking. The four basic methods of estimating reliability and the type of information each provides are shown in Table 9.3.

TEST-RETEST METHOD

The test-retest method requires administering the same form of the test to the same group with some intervening time interval. The time between the two administrations may be just a few days or several years. The length of the time interval should fit the type of interpretation to be made from the results. Thus, if we are interested in using test scores only to group students for more effective learning, short-term stability may be sufficient. On the other hand, if we are attempting to predict vocational success or make some other long-range predictions, we would desire evidence of stability over a period of years.

Test-retest reliability coefficients are influenced both by errors within the measurement procedure and by the day-to-day stability of the students' responses. Thus, longer time periods between testing will result in lower reliability coefficients, due to the greater changes in the students. In reporting test-retest reliability coefficients, then, it is important to include the time interval. For example, a report might state, "The stability of test scores obtained on the same form over a three-month period was .90." This makes it possible to determine the extent to which the reliability data are significant for a particular interpretation.

EQUIVALENT-FORMS METHOD

With this method, two equivalent forms of a test (also called alternate forms or parallel forms) are administered to the same group during the same testing session. The test forms are equivalent in the sense that they are built to measure the same abilities (that is, they are built to the same table of specifications), but for determining reliability it is also important that they be constructed independently. When this is the case, the reliability coefficient indicates the adequacy of the test sample. That is, a high reliability coefficient would indicate that the two independent samples are apparently measuring the same thing. A low reliability coefficient, of course, would indicate that the two forms are measuring different behavior and that therefore both samples of items are questionable.

Table 9.3. *Methods of Estimating Reliability*

METHOD	TYPE OF INFORMATION PROVIDED
Test-retest method	The stability of test scores over some given period of time
Equivalent-forms method	The consistency of the test scores over different forms of the test (i.e., different samples of items)
Test-retest with equivalent forms	The consistency of test scores over *both* a time interval and different forms of the test
Internal-consistency methods	The consistency of test scores over different parts of the test

Note: Scorer reliability should also be considered when evaluating the responses to *supply-type* items (e.g., essay tests). This is typically done by having the test papers scored independently by two scorers and then correlating the two sets of scores. Agreement among scorers, however, is not a substitute for the methods of estimating reliability shown in the table.

Reliability coefficients determined by this method take into account errors within the measurement procedure and consistency over different samples of items, but they do not include the day-to-day stability of the students' responses.

TEST-RETEST METHOD WITH EQUIVALENT FORMS

This is a combination of both of the above methods. Here, two different forms of the same test are administered with an intervening time interval. This is the most demanding estimate of reliability, since it takes into account all possible sources of variation. The reliability coefficient reflects errors within the testing procedure, consistency over different samples of items, and the day-to-day stability of the students' responses. For most purposes this is probably the most useful type of reliability, since it enables us to estimate how generalizable the test results are over the various conditions. A high reliability coefficient obtained by this method would indicate that a test score represents not only present test performance but also what test performance is likely to be at another time or on a different sample of equivalent items.

INTERNAL-CONSISTENCY METHODS

These methods require only a single administration of a test. One procedure, the *split-half* method, involves scoring the odd items and the even items separately and correlating the two sets of scores. This correlation coefficient indicates the degree to which the two arbitrarily selected halves of the test provide the same results. Thus, it reports on the internal consistency of the test. Like the equivalent-forms method, this procedure takes into account errors within the testing procedure and consistency over different samples of items, but it omits the day-to-day stability of the students' responses.

Since the correlation coefficient based on the odd and even items indicates the relationship between two halves of the test, the reliability coefficient for the total test is determined by applying the Spearman-Brown prophecy formula. A simplified version of this formula is as follows:

$$\text{Reliability of total test} = \frac{2 \times \text{reliability for } \frac{1}{2} \text{ test}}{1 + \text{reliability for } \frac{1}{2} \text{ test}}$$

Thus, if we obtained a correlation coefficient of .60 for two halves of a test, the reliability for the total test would be computed as follows:

$$\text{Reliability of total test} = \frac{2 \times .60}{1 + .60} = \frac{1.20}{1.60} = .75$$

This application of the Spearman-Brown formula makes clear a useful principle of test reliability; the reliability of a test can be increased by lengthening it. The above formula shows how much reliability will increase when the length of the test is doubled. Application of the formula, however, assumes that the test is lengthened by adding items like those already in the test.

Probably the simplest means of estimating the reliability of test scores from a single administration of a test is to use Kuder-Richardson Formula 21. This formula requires just three types of information: (1) the number of items in the test, (2) the mean (or arithmetic average), and (3) the standard deviation. Since we learned a short-cut method for estimating the standard deviation in the last chapter, this formula is especially easy to apply to classroom achievement tests. A simplified version of the formula, taken from a bulletin by Diederich (1973) is presented below. Although this formula omits a minor correction factor, it is satisfactory for use with most classroom tests.

$$\text{Reliability estimate } (KR21) = 1 - \frac{M\,(K - M)}{K(s^2)}$$

where K = the number of items in the test; M = the mean of the test scores; and s = the standard deviation of the test scores.

Although this formula may look a bit formidable at first glance, we simply insert the quantities called for and apply our arithmetic skills. For example, if $K = 40$, $M = 29$, and $s = 4.5$ (from the data in Table 8.2), the reliability estimate would be computed as follows:

$$\text{Reliability} = 1 - \frac{29\,(40 - 29)}{40\,(4.5^2)}$$

$$= 1 - \frac{29 \times 11}{40 \times 20.25}$$

$$= 1 - .39$$

$$= .61$$

Thus, the reliability estimate for our 40-item test is .61. We might now ask if the reliability of these test scores is high or low. As with validity coefficients, there are two readily usable bench marks for evaluating a reliability coefficient. First, we can compare it to the extreme degrees of reliability that it is possible to obtain. A complete lack of reliability would be indicated by a coefficient of .00, and perfect positive reliability would be indicated by a coefficient of 1.00. This provides a general framework within which to view a particular reliability coefficient. Second, and probably more important, we can compare our reliability coefficient with those that are usually obtained for achievement tests. The reported reliabilities for standardized achievement tests are frequently over .90 when Kuder-Richardson formulas are used. The reliability coefficients for classroom tests typically range between .60 and .80 (Diederich, 1973). When we view our reliability coefficient in this light, we might consider it to be rather low.

Kuder-Richardson Formula 21 provides a conservative estimate of reliability. Since it is based on the consistency of student response from item to item, it tends to provide smaller correlation coefficients than the split-half method.

Internal-consistency methods are used widely because they require that the test be administered only once. They should not be used with speeded tests, however, because a spuriously high reliability estimate will result. If speed is an important factor in the testing (that is, if the students do not have time to attempt all the items), other methods should be used to estimate reliability.

STANDARD ERROR OF MEASUREMENT

The standard error of measurement is an especially useful way of expressing test reliability because it indicates the amount of error to allow for when interpreting individual test scores. The standard error is derived from a reliability coefficient by means of the following formula:

$$\text{Standard error of measurement} = s\sqrt{1 - r_{\prime\prime}}$$

where s = the standard deviation and $r_{\prime\prime}$ = the reliability coefficient. In applying this formula to the Kuder-Richardson reliability estimate of .61 obtained earlier ($s = 4.5$), the following results would be obtained:

$$\begin{aligned}\text{Standard error of measurement} &= 4.5\sqrt{1 - .61}\\ &= 4.5\sqrt{.39}\\ &= 4.5 \times .63\\ &= 2.8\end{aligned}$$

Although the standard error of measurement is easily computed, for most informal achievement testing a satisfactory approximation of this measure can be obtained from the length of the test. The following table, prepared by Paul Diederich (1973), provides an estimate of the amount of error to be expected for tests of different lengths. The standard-error column shows how many points we must add to, and subtract from, an individual's test score in order to obtain "reasonable limits" for estimating her true score (that is, a score free of error).

NUMBER OF ITEMS IN THE TEST	STANDARD ERROR
less than 24	2
24–47	3
48–89	4
90–109	5
110–129	6
130–150	7

If we were using a 40-item test, as in our earlier example, the standard error would be approximately 3 score points. Thus, if a given student scored 35 on this test, his *score band,* for establishing reasonable limits, would range from 32 (35 − 3) to 38 (35 + 3). In other words, we could be reasonably sure that the score band of 32 to 38 included the student's true score (statistically, there are two chances out of three that it does). These estimated standard errors of test scores provide a rough indication of the amount of error to expect in tests of different lengths, and they highlight the importance of allowing for error during test interpretation. If we view test performance in terms of score bands, we are not likely to overinterpret small differences between test scores.

The previous table also illustrates that the proportionate amount of error in a test score becomes smaller as the test becomes longer. Note, for example, that a test of 50 items has a standard error of 4 and a test of 100 items has a standard error of 5. Although the length of the test is doubled, the amount of error is increased by only one fourth. This is in harmony with the principle stated earlier: longer tests provide more reliable results.

For the test user, the standard error of measurement is probably more useful than the reliability coefficient. Although reliability coefficients can be used in evaluating the quality of a test and in comparing the relative merits of different tests, the standard error of measurement is directly applicable to the interpretation of individual test scores.

RELIABILITY OF CRITERION-REFERENCED MASTERY TESTS

As we noted earlier, the traditional methods of estimating reliability require score variability and are therefore useful mainly with norm-referenced tests. A number of attempts have been made to modify or create procedures for estimating the reliability of criterion-referenced mastery tests, but a satisfactory method has yet to be proposed. Until adequate procedures are provided, we will have to rely on care in test construction to assure reliable results. In general, the likelihood of reliable test scores is increased by constructing test items that are free of defects and by using an adequate number of items for each instructional objective to be measured. If the objective is very specific, a decision concerning mastery might be made with as few as five items. For most mastery-nonmastery decisions, however, ten items would be more desirable. Since the results on criterion-referenced mastery tests are typically interpreted *by objective,* it is the number of items measuring each objective that is important, rather than the total length of the test.

Additional Reading

American Psychological Association, *Standards for Educational and Psychological Tests.* Washington, D.C., 1974. See the sections on validity (pp. 25–48) and reliability (pp. 48–55).

ANASTASI, A., *Psychological Testing* (4th ed.), Chaps. 5 and 6. New York: Macmillan Publishing Co., Inc., 1976. Describes standard types of reliability and validity.

CRONBACH, L. J., "Test Validation," in *Educational Measurement* (2nd ed.), ed. R. L. Thorndike, Chap. 14. Washington, D.C.: American Council on Education, 1971. A detailed treatment of validity, with emphasis on educational testing.

DIEDERICH, P. B., *Short-Cut Statistics for Teacher-Made Tests.* Princeton, N.J.: Educational Testing Service, 1973. Presents simplified methods of analyzing test scores and estimating reliability.

GRONLUND, N. E., *Measurement and Evaluation in Teaching* (3rd ed.), Chaps. 4 and 5. New York: Macmillan Publishing Co., Inc., 1976. Basic types of reliability and validity are described in relation to educational testing.

HELMSTADTER, G. C., *Principles of Psychological Measurement,* Chaps. 3, 4 and 6. New York: Appleton-Century-Crofts, 1964. Clear, comprehensive descriptions of reliability, content validity, and construct validity.

POPHAM, W. J., *Educational Evaluation,* Chap. 7. Englewood Cliffs, N.J.: Prentice-Hall, Inc., 1975. See especially the discussion of reliability and validity of criterion-referenced tests (pp. 151–60).

STANLEY, J. C., "Reliability," in *Educational Measurement* (2nd ed.), ed. R. L. Thorndike, Chap. 13. Washington, D.C.: American Council on Education, 1971. A detailed and technical treatment of reliability.

Index